Man of Christian Action

CANON JOHN COLLINS
— the man and his work

Man of Christian Action

CANON JOHN COLLINS
— the man and his work

Edited by
Ian Henderson

LUTTERWORTH PRESS
GUILDFORD AND LONDON

First published 1976

ISBN 0 7188 2271 4

COPYRIGHT © 1976 CHRISTIAN ACTION

Printed in Great Britain by
Cox & Wyman Limited,
London, Fakenham and Reading

Contents

List of Illustrations and Acknowledgements

The publishers wish to express their gratitude to the following for the photographs reproduced in this volume: Mr. E. Ryle-Hodges for no. 1; Scottish Studios for no. 2; the *Morning Star* for no. 3; Mr. C. Schwarz for nos. 4 and 6; the Associated Press, Ltd. for no. 5; the *Evening Standard* for no. 9; the Keystone Press Agency, Ltd. for no. 10; and the United Nations for no. 11.

Editor's Preface

This book was conceived for the not especially significant reason that Canon John Collins in 1975 attained the age of three score years and ten. It might have been written equally well to mark any one of several other occasions in the life of this remarkable man and the movement he founded. However, as both refuse to adhere to a tidy pattern of behaviour and relish the unpredictable and the unexpected, a seventieth birthday tribute seemed as good a way as any of putting on record some assessments of John Collins and of the causes he has espoused. It also invited some considerations at a philosophical and theological level as to why anyone, Christian or humanist, should bother about the state of human society.

John Collins has based his life on the belief that as a Christian, a priest and a student of the New Testament he ought to be involved in a particular style of social witness which he maintains most persuasively is the implication of the gospel to which he devoted the first part of his adult life as a scholar. One characteristic of this understanding of Christian action is that it ought to be undertaken by Christians of all traditions – John Collins is one of the most practical exponents of ecumenism of our generation – and by the many thousands of thoughtful people who stand outside the fellowship of the Christian church but who find the life and teaching of Jesus of Nazareth strangely compelling.

From the beginning, John Collins was joined by such people. Perhaps the late Sir Victor Gollancz was one of the first. But there are many others who bear witness to the effect that John Collins had on them. One of the most interesting observations made in this book by an agnostic friend and erstwhile colleague of his, Mervyn Jones, concerns John's role as a priest in the Campaign for Nuclear Disarmament which brought together for common action a very wide cross-section of people and philosophies. He says that he now wishes that John had talked more rather than less theology at CND committees.

In this book there are a number of contributions by distinguished humanists whose paths have crossed with that of John Collins.

J. B. Priestley who was also involved in CND opens the book with a personal appreciation of John based on close friendship and a working partnership. This is followed by theological papers on Christian Action, the movement which John Collins founded and which from very early days involved two of the authors of these papers. One of these is Father Tom Corbishley, one of the most distinguished members of the Society of Jesus in this generation, whose tragic death occurred while this volume was in preparation. The other is Edward Carpenter, now Dean of Westminster. The section begins with the contribution of another clerical author, Joseph Robinson, who gives an appreciation of John's long and fruitful association with St. Paul's Cathedral where his courage, integrity and innovatory genius not only helped re-think the role of cathedrals in the church of today but also aided the growth of the ecumenical movement.

The Earl of Longford and Sir Richard Acland have also been associated with John Collins and Christian Action for over thirty years. They are both practising Christians who have worked out their discipleship in the world of politics and public life and who both, at certain moments of their career, had to part company with their colleagues on grounds of conscience. For Frank Longford this meant resignation from the Government, for Richard Acland leaving Parliament. Sir Richard in his essay has some critical but challenging things to say about the course which Christian Action has taken in the last three decades, and hints at a route for the future.

The other essays in this volume are all about aspects of work which have merited the attention and energy of John Collins. From the earliest days of the nationalist regime in South Africa, John and Christian Action saw apartheid as an affront to the Christian conscience. This at first involved public support for Christian leaders in that country who voiced the protest of conscience. One of these is Bishop Trevor Huddleston who writes about those early days of John's concern with South Africa. Later, the Defence and Aid Fund which John founded became a large international organization attracting the support of several governments including that of Sweden. Per Wästberg as a Swedish supporter of International Defence and Aid writes about this development. My own years as a staff member of Christian Action were mostly occupied with our work for homeless families and single homeless people, known as Homeless in Britain. In my essay I endeavour not only to describe this work but to discuss the greater question of Christian objectives in social work.

The other movement which engaged John's enthusiasm and earned for him at once great public attention and great public misunderstanding was the Campaign for Nuclear Disarmament. The Campaign of course goes on and the Bomb is still, alas, with us. But CND was more than a movement; it was the mood of a generation, and its style of campaigning profoundly affected all kinds of protest movements for the next decade. In the context of British democracy John Collins has always been a firm supporter of non-violent, constitutional protest. Mervyn Jones writes on CND and John's days as Chairman, while another close personal friend, Jacquetta Hawkes (in private life, Mrs J. B. Priestley) discusses the limits of public protest.

The last essay in this volume is unlike the others although it has affinities with the theologians whose contributions appear earlier. It is by the philosopher and novelist Iris Murdoch, who was also involved in CND and other movements led or supported by John Collins. In her contribution Miss Murdoch discusses in some technical detail the basis of a viable moral philosophy, relating her case to the philosophy of art.

Finally an African poet, Raymond Kunene, who has been a leading member of the African nationalist movement and lives in exile from his native land, pays a special personal tribute to John Collins in a poem which is based on the rich symbolism of his people.

Although so many of these essays review inevitably the recent past and things achieved, the reader will discern a constant feeling after new directions for Christian Action and the movements with which it is associated. Happily and fortunately for Christian Action, John Collins is still actively involved as our President. This volume may remind him of what he has achieved and what lies ahead to challenge us all.

Ian Henderson

JOHN COLLINS
A Portrait

J. B. Priestley

This is a remarkable book about a remarkable man. The book is remarkable because it covers so much varied ground. The man is remarkable because of course he covers the same ground. I don't propose to go over it; our contributors here will be doing that and, as public speakers know only too well, nobody is more irritating than the chairman who makes their points for them in an introduction. What I can do best in this place is to write about John Collins in terms of my acquaintance and then close friendship with him. I may have to bring myself in rather a lot, but then I am an old hand at this. However, unless a fairly convincing sketch-portrait of John Collins emerges, I shall have failed here – and the fact that nearly everything else seems to be failing will not console me.

I first met Canon Collins when he was appointed Chairman of CND. And I will admit at once that I missed the point about him. What is the point? It is that not only is he an unusual man but also he is an *unusual* unusual man. What do I mean by this? I mean that most unusual men are going to prove it at first sight. They will show you at once they are extraordinary fellows, far removed from the common run. The *unusual* unusual man (very rare) makes no such effort and has not this effect in mind. He just goes on being himself, leaving you to discover gradually his unique and rewarding quality. And I say again that such men are rare, and I say it at the end of a long lifetime after meeting all manner of folk.

I didn't dislike this Canon Collins – how could I? – but I wasn't impressed. He was not my idea of a capable chairman. He seemed to me altogether too patient, easy-going, good-natured. But then I had always been a tough chairman. (Chairing an international conference in Paris, I was challenged to a duel by a South American windbag, who had bored me beyond endurance.) There were two or three members of this committee, from out of town (I think) and certainly not the most effective campaigners, who wasted a good deal of our time because they were in love with the sounds of their own voices. I would have dealt harshly with these types. Canon Collins never turned upon them a single frown. Not the hint of a rebuke came from him. This seemed to me not good enough. Was this the sort of chairman we needed?

As a matter of fact, it was, and I had been wrong. (I am often wrong, apparently unlike almost everybody else.) For this kind of committee, meeting regularly and consisting of very different types, my sort of chairmanship would have been a disaster. This tolerant, smiling Canon Collins, never losing his temper yet somehow getting through the agenda, was just the man we needed. I descended from some idiotic height of conceit and dogmatism to seek and welcome this man's company and to consider him more closely. He was, I began to realize, no ordinary rebellious cleric. He was not just another eager reformer and enthusiastic protester. I had moved for a fairly long time in company along the left wing and was well acquainted with the sort of men and women who toiled and sometimes flourished there. This John Collins, now a friend, was able to feel at home among them, but he was very different from most of them. The unusual man began to emerge.

To begin with, he was not really an idealogue. (And now I consider ideology one of the curses of our age.) Instead of referring people and their needs, hopes and fears to a system, making them fit in whether they liked it or not, he saw them as fellow human beings, entangled in this life of ours, bewildered, perhaps feeling frustrated, busy fearing or modestly hoping. And without this attitude of mind, there can be no such thing as liberal democracy, at best a fading dream. My friend John never set himself up as a propagandist of liberal democracy – in point of fact he went much deeper than that – but clearly he behaved as if such a thing existed or ought to exist. And obviously it was all the same to him if it wore a black face or a pinky-white one.

To see people in these terms and then to be at their disposal demands not only good feeling but also enormous patience – a great deal more than I could supply, outside my own work. As friendship grew closer and revealed more and more of ordinary

2

daily living, I appreciated and marvelled at this fund of patience, quite beyond anything I could ever muster. However, I soon discovered that he had one important ally. This was a notable sense of humour, rarely found among eager reformers, sharp protesters, rebels, challengers of establishment complacency, who are often nothing if solemnly humourless. But it will not do simply to clap our hands at the idea of a sense of humour. As some admired writers have shown us, a sense of humour can be cruel, negative and life-defeating, usually because these very writers have felt themselves to be defeated in some deeply inward campaign. But (thank heaven!) there is also a kind, positive, life-enhancing sense of humour, smiling through that patience already noted, the friendly laugh at the end of a long tiring day. And if my friend John Collins hasn't that sense of humour, then I have learnt nothing about human nature. In fact he has it in abundance. Clerical gentlemen, I am sorry to add, are often notorious for loud empty laughs. I have never known John Collins to offer me one. His laughs are full, relating to reality.

Nevertheless, he too is a parson. (I have even had long arguments with him about theology, the two of us never arriving anywhere together.) Not only that, but he is *very much* a parson, or – should we say? – a priest, deeply aware of his duties and responsibilities as a priest. This side of him is unknown to the general mass of the public, taking newspapers as their guides. Most of them in fact entertain the wrong image of him. They know about South Africa or the Aldermaston march or an occasional militant sermon, but they do not know that this is also a man who takes both his cathedral, to which he is devoted, and also his pastoral duties very seriously indeed. There are times when I wonder if the church really understands John Collins very much better than the news editor of the Daily Splash, who sees him as a possible story now and again. I have never discussed this subject with my friend – we have much else to talk about – but if the church does not understand him, then I must add that I don't understand the church. It is rather like a man who, with a certain course to run, leaves a racehorse in its stable and uses circus ponies.

Of one thing I am certain. Sustaining everything this man has done and does, the whole wide range of his activities, his rich response to every human appeal, is a deep living faith. Perhaps I move in the wrong circles, but it is a fact that I rarely meet a *real Christian*. We have one here, one secure in his belief and prepared to put it into practice. Now I repeat what I said earlier, that this is an *unusual* unusual man. And it was a fine idea to devote a book to him. I have had to write many introductions – they go along with my trade – but this is very special, coming out of affection but also to be regarded as a privilege. Now . . . read on.

PART ONE

CHRISTIAN ACTION AND
THEOLOGY

1 MAN AND CATHEDRAL

Joseph Robinson

When I moved to St. Paul's to take office as a minor canon of the cathedral in January 1956 I had never met John Collins. This may seem strange in that a man would normally expect to see, and be seen by all the members of a cathedral chapter before taking up such an appointment. I had in fact been interviewed by the dean and chapter some months before, but John Collins was not present at the interview. He was in hospital and was away from the cathedral convalescing for several months.

So John Collins was the last canon of the cathedral whom I met. This fact is particularly vivid in my memory because in the months after I accepted the minor canonry and was preparing to move to St. Paul's, the cathedral was frequently a topic of conversation with people I met. I was a curate in a parish in the diocese of London and so was living and working among people who had some knowledge of, and interest in St. Paul's. As they spoke to me about the cathedral, the name of John Collins was often mentioned and I began to realize that he was a man who was a public figure and a centre of controversy.

On the one hand I happened to meet a young priest whom I had known as an undergraduate. He told me how fortunate I was to have the opportunity of working with John Collins. He had known him during the war, when he had been serving in the R.A.F., and had met John as his station chaplain. He spoke most enthusiastically, in glowing terms, of all that John had done and in particular of how he had broken down all barriers of class and rank on his station and created a magnificent Christian fellowship among the men. I had served in the R.A.F. before going up to the university and knew enough of those barriers of class and rank to realize that anyone who could do anything such as my

7

friend claimed for John Collins, must be a very remarkable person indeed.

On the other hand, some of the older clergy, men who had served in the diocese of London for many years, spoke with much greater reserve about him. This was not limited to John Collins; some of them had very little enthusiasm for St. Paul's. They felt that its position as a national church got in the way of its function as mother church of the diocese of London and, in effect, they had no cathedral in anything other than name, but always somewhere amongst their complaints the name of John Collins would crop up. He was a man who in their view was simply using his position at St. Paul's to disseminate left-wing political propaganda, and therefore was taking the cathedral even further away from what they wanted it to be. Usually the point was put emphatically, with that degree of heat which indicated that they strongly disagreed with his point of view. After this I was both intrigued and somewhat apprehensive of meeting John Collins. He sounded a formidable character.

Then when I had arrived at St. Paul's and was settling in, I didn't see very much of John at first. I was given duties which brought me into very little direct contact with him. So again even at St. Paul's my first impression of him was through the impact that he had made on others. I found that impression to be both similar to and also different from my earlier impressions. There was the same sharp cleavage of opinion about his views; he polarized opinion. There were those who were strongly in favour of what he was saying and doing. There were others who equally strongly disapproved, especially of what they called bringing politics into the pulpit of St. Paul's. But at St. Paul's there was a noticeable difference. The heat and anger with which such sentiments had usually been expressed were absent. Rather there was, even among those who were most resolutely opposed to his views, a clearly detectable liking for John Collins as a man. I gained a very clear opinion that no matter how greatly the views and opinions expressed by John Collins were disliked and even detested, it was quite impossible for anyone who knew him personally to do anything other than like him as a man. He was clearly a character of singular attractiveness who was able to create a happy human relationship even with those who were divided from him in outlook and principle. That was the judgement I reached from living and working at St. Paul's for a short time. I remained at St. Paul's for twelve years and during that time I came to know John well and to count him as a friend, but I never found that I needed to go back in any way on that judgement. One could disagree with John Collins, and most people at St. Paul's did disagree with him over some issue or other, but disagreement never broke or even impaired affection. He was so human, so likeable, and so Christian.

It is often said that it is children who help people to get to know each other. They establish contact far more quickly than adults. This is true in my case. The first really personal contact I had with John Collins was through our children. When we moved to St. Paul's we had one son and he was soon joined by a sister. The two younger Collins sons were only a little older than my children and they soon became firm friends and good playmates. The children were very ingenious in creating games to play in the rather confined area of Amen Court. They enjoyed themselves immensely and entertained each other. Sometimes they could be noisy and incur the disapproval of some of the other residents, and then the Robinsons and the Collins's felt drawn together. In fact both John and Diana Collins went out of their way to be good neighbours and friends to the family of a junior and younger colleague. And not only to the Robinsons. There were a few other children living in Amen Court and all of them were made welcome in the Collins's house. I remember in particular that, while the children were young enough to enjoy it, John Collins always had a firework party on or near November 5, and all the other children living in Amen Court were invited. Such parties were real red letter days in the lives of all the children and are an instance of the kindness that John and Diana Collins showed to us and their other neighbours.

The point in mentioning this is that a personal incident of this kind, trivial though it may be, conveys far more clearly than many words something of that quality of friendship and good neighbourliness that both John and Diana Collins brought to Amen Court. John had himself at an earlier stage in his career been a minor canon at St. Paul's, and life at the cathedral at that time was strictly formal. For example, until 1940 all the cathedral clergy wore clerical frock coats and top hats on Sundays. The war brought an end to that and probably to many of the old ways. Dean Matthews often said that the wartime blitz and the creation of a band of volunteer firefighters to guard the cathedral against air attack, created (or at least revealed) a spirit of friendship around the cathedral which had not been evident before. So after the war was

9

over, many of those who had helped in the firefighting joined together to found a new organization, the Friends of St. Paul's, with the object of continuing the new spirit of friendship in the future. What the Friends of St. Paul's set out to do for the cathedral in general, the coming of John and Diana Collins to Amen Court in 1948 did for the life of the Amen Court community. They set out to create a spirit of friendship and good neighbourliness which crossed and broke down all barriers of rank. This made a great deal of difference to life in a close-knit community which was hierarchically structured, and therefore could be at times very rank-conscious, both from above and below.

So far I have been offering a personal impression of human contacts with John Collins. That is important because it witnesses to a dimension of his work at St. Paul's which was, and I am sure still is important in itself, and to which John himself attached importance. Yet important as that may be, it is not the main part of John Collins' work at St. Paul's. That work involves the use he has made of the office of canon residentiary, which he has held since 1948. In discussing that use, I am somewhat at a disadvantage. I was never a residentiary canon at St. Paul's and so never attended chapter meetings or took any part in the decision-making process of the governing body of the cathedral. However I can offer some comment, as one who was a servant of the dean and chapter of St. Paul's for a considerable time and who had experience, since leaving St. Paul's for Canterbury, of the working of a dean and chapter.

One of the great attractions of the office of canon residentiary is that the holder of the office is left a considerable amount of freedom to decide in which way he will use it. The bare official work of the canonry is lighter than that of many other jobs. A canon must be 'in residence' for a part of the year (at St. Paul's three months), during which time he is expected to attend the daily services, preach at the afternoon service on Sundays and exercise a general oversight on the day-to-day running of the cathedral. He must also attend the meetings of the chapter and be responsible for putting into action such decisions of the chapter as relate to the particular aspect of the work of the cathedral which has been allotted to him. At St. Paul's there are three ancient offices, Precentor, Treasurer and Chancellor, and each of the residentiary canons (other than the Archdeacon of London) is expected to undertake one of them.

The Precentor looks after the music and the choir. The Treasurer is concerned for the fabric of the cathedral and all those whose duty it is to maintain it in good repair. The Chancellor is responsible for the cathedral library. John Collins has held each of these offices; each demands some administrative work from a canon but leaves him with some free time and energy to work and exercise his own gifts in the way which seems most useful to himself and to others. So the tradition arose that a canonry was often reserved for a scholarly priest who could use it to read and write. The position of St. Paul's in the centre of London which ensures that the cathedral attracts large congregations to its services means that many of the canons have also been notable preachers, but essentially each canon is free to work in his own way. This creates a unique opportunity for a man who has something to say or do. It may also create its own tensions. A gifted canon will not lack work. Calls are likely to be made on his time from many quarters. Any piece of work he takes up is likely to absorb all the time and energy he can give it. The problem comes in allocating time and energy to the various calls, and the tensions arise as between cathedral-based work and that which is done outside.

It was these very opportunities for developing his own work which led John Collins to accept the offer of a canonry at St. Paul's. He believed he had a work to do in developing 'Christian Action', and he believed that he had been sent to St. Paul's to do that work. Consequently he used the opportunities offered by its pulpit to make known as widely as possible the causes espoused by 'Christian Action' and the attitudes to public issues which 'Christian Action' adopted. He was eminently successful in his use of the pulpit in this way. For the most part his preaching did not draw great crowds, but he did catch the attention of the press and his sermons were widely reported by them and raised much comment. His sermons often dealt with controversial contemporary issues and displayed a clear uncompromising point of view which at times infuriated those who did not agree with him. He made no secret of the fact that he was a socialist and, while being very far from equating the socialist state with the kingdom of heaven, found it very difficult to believe that the policies of any other of the parties acting in British politics could advance the cause of Christianity. This impression was conveyed to many of his hearers and was the basis of that reserve and hostility towards him of which I have written earlier.

But for the most part, party political issues did not figure directly in his preaching. His concern was what he considered to be the big social and moral issues of the day. Three I remember as being pre-eminent: the demand to abolish capital punishment; the demand that Great Britain should give up atomic weapons and have no part in the testing of atomic bombs; and the evil of racism in general, and the system of apartheid in South Africa in particular. These three issues above all others constituted for him a call to the Christian conscience of the nation. He could see no way in which Christians could argue or debate these issues. For him they could only be condemned, and such condemnation he uttered as frequently, tirelessly and uncompromisingly as any Old Testament prophet. To the criticism that they were political issues best left to statesmen, he replied that in a democracy it was the duty of all leaders of opinion to make their views heard and felt on issues which concerned the moral and spiritual well-being of the nation. To the criticism that they were not the kind of spiritual issues which demanded treatment by a preacher, he replied that all issues concerned with the material and social well-being of people must have a spiritual dimension. In many sermons he repeated a quotation from the Russian author Berdyaeev: 'Bread for myself is a material matter, but bread for my brother is a spiritual matter'. Looking back now, it seems amazing that sermons condemning the practice of capital punishment and the system of apartheid in South Africa could have been regarded as being so controversial. Things have moved on, and the great body of educated opinion in our country on these matters stands today where John Collins stood twenty years ago. Only the future historian will be able to say precisely how much of the change of opinion that has taken place is owing to the sermons of John Collins. All I can say now is that they clearly had a considerable influence.

The other aspect of John's use of the pulpit of St. Paul's concerned the great preachers whom he invited to fill it. Apart from the minor canons whom he regularly invited to preach, the men he usually invited were religious leaders associated with the causes in which he was interested. John was often able to get well-known men to occupy the pulpit who drew very large congregations. One of the first I remember was Paul Robeson, the negro singer, who came to St. Paul's one Sunday night not to preach but to sing. A vast congregation came to hear him. At the time that Trevor Huddleston returned to this country from his work in Johannesburg, he also occupied the pulpit of St. Paul's and must have had a congregation of two thousand people. Such congregations made the great cathedral come alive. They demonstrated its functioning as Sir Christopher Wren must have intended it to function. One such occasion was more outstanding than all the others. Indeed it must be one of the great days in the whole history of St. Paul's. That was when Martin Luther King preached at Sunday afternoon evensong. This service which took place at 3.15 p.m. was usually the least well attended of all the Sunday services. English people do not take kindly to attending church almost immediately after lunch! Yet on that day, even before the service began, every seat in the cathedral was occupied and vast numbers of people were standing in the aisles in every part of the building. I do not ever remember having seen the cathedral so full of people. Dr. King had not arrived by the time the service began as his plane had been delayed and we were rather concerned about disappointing such a great crowd of people. However he arrived during the service and preached a magnificent sermon that must have lasted an hour. That meant that the great crowd of people standing in the aisles were on their feet for over two hours. Many of them were young people, probably unfamiliar with the solemn stateliness of cathedral worship; but they remained quiet, attentive and reverent throughout the very long service. It was a memorable, more a moving occasion. I can still remember the text from which Dr. King preached. So John Collins has used St. Paul's to proclaim his message. In so doing he has followed in the steps of many canons before him who have used that pulpit in their own way. Yet he has not just taken what St. Paul's has to offer. He has also brought to it what he has to give, and that offering includes some very memorable occasions and some very large congregations.

I wrote above that a canon is free to decide how he will use much of his time. If he chooses or feels compelled to devote that time to important causes which demand all that he can give, then tension is likely to develop between conflicting interests. A commitment to a movement or group of people demands regular, constant attention, and such attention can be sustained by a canon only at times. Then along comes one of those months in the year when he is 'in residence' and immediately the cathedral makes much heavier demands on his time and energies. There are services to be attended daily. There are administrative matters which need decisions, some of them quite trivial in comparison with the great issues of the world outside, but still demanding time. Is the canon to withdraw from his interests and activities outside the cathedral at such periods, or ought he to keep them going as best he can? This is a problem which affects all cathedral canons. For John Collins with the ever growing daily pressures of 'Christian Action' so dependent upon him, and with many other claims being made on his time from so many important causes, it must have been a nightmare.

I remember one occasion when I was new at St. Paul's and John was in residence. The time for evensong was approaching fast and the canon had not appeared in the cathedral. Then a message was brought across from his house to ask us to begin without him. It was at the time when he was conducting a campaign against capital punishment and he had in his study the father of a man who had been found guilty of murder and condemned to die. In the light of that man's problems, he felt he could not break off the interview and go to evensong. This kind of conflict of duties arose from time to time and John was always quite clear in his own mind that when they did, the routine work must take second place to the need that had arisen. The impression could be given that he neglected the duties of the cathedral, and some of those who were less burdened with the pressures of other work criticized him for neglecting St. Paul's. John was, I think, at times sensitive to the accusation, and may have been rather hurt by it. With the job that a residentiary canon is given to do and the work he is expected to create for and around himself, it is a charge which in some way can be levelled against any residentiary canon anywhere who is worth his salt. There is bound to be some conflict between various kinds of work in which he is involved. Few residentiary canons anywhere can have had the expectations laid upon them, or faced the demands that have been made upon John Collins. He felt that he had been sent to St. Paul's in order to do a particular job, namely to make 'Christian Action' a force in the church and in the land. As things worked out that often meant responding to human needs such as the need of poor African refugees. John Collins being the man he was, and is, could only respond to the problem in one way: to serve what he clearly saw to be the greater need and to accept whatever criticism might come from those who saw things in a different way.

If John was sensitive to the charge of being indifferent to St. Paul's, it was, I believe, because he had in reality a deep and abiding love for it. He served for a brief time in the earlier part of his ministry as a minor canon at St. Paul's and had at that time fallen in love with the cathedral. This was part of the reason why he welcomed the offer of the canonry. It is quite impossible to live and work in St. Paul's, to see all the great crowds of people who visit it, to take part in all the things that happen there without becoming imbued with a deep sense of its place in the national life and the real feeling of love and respect that so many people have for it. To be associated with St. Paul's is to serve one of the great religious institutions of our nation with a place in the past of our people, and with opportunities just as great for influence and service in the present and future. Any priest who is privileged to work at St. Paul's comes to love it and I believe this has certainly applied to John Collins. He returned to St. Paul's with his vision of using the cathedral as a focus for preaching the Christian message to our world. In the nineteenth century St. Paul's had been noted for that kind of leadership, and John felt that he could help it to exercise the same kind of leadership once more in the twentieth century. This was the reason why he was so delighted when the cathedral was filled to hear the preachers whom he had invited to it. He too has a great sense of the place of St. Paul's in the national life and he welcomed sharing in the great national occasions that have taken place in the cathedral since 1948. He was canon in residence when the restored High Altar was reconsecrated by the Bishop of London in the presence of the Queen and Prince Philip in 1958, and took an active part in all the preparation that went on for that service. On another occasion, the service to mark the inauguration of the Independent State of Sierra Leone was held at St. Paul's very largely because of John's presence on the chapter, and he was invited to preach at the service.

Only once can I remember a service when John seemed to be out of sympathy with what was being done. This was the Remembrance Sunday service when it was the custom for the Lord Mayor of London together with many of the aldermen and city officers to attend the cathedral in state. Although he had been an R.A.F. chaplain, John had since the war become a firmly committed pacifist. He felt that the customary way of marking Remembrance Sunday with military parades and ceremonies was too nationalistic for a world which ought increasingly to be seeing its future in international terms. He wished therefore that Remembrance Day should strike a note of forgiveness and reconciliation rather than one of national pride which might only re-open old wounds and reactivate old hatreds. It fell to him as canon in residence to preach at the service on several years and he made his point with characteristic vigour and uncompromising clarity. His aim and purpose were good but some of the congregation were hurt and offended by the way in which they considered that he had trampled on their deeply held feelings. Those sermons undoubtedly alienated some people from him, but a prophet must speak in his own way and John never flinched from facing the criticism that might follow.

In concluding these reminiscences I can say that I count it a privilege and a joy to have known John and Diana Collins. Living as a neighbour of theirs in Amen Court for twelve years, I came to know them as belonging to those finest of all persons: those who care truly and deeply for and about people. They wanted to help all who came into their lives and needed help. They also wanted to make the world a more caring place. This may sound solemn and a bit pompous. If so then it is failing to convey the right impression because with all his caring John Collins is the least pompous of men. When I worked with him he was gay and full of fun and yet had a quite remarkable capacity for dealing seriously with most important matters, quite often matters which inherently had much sadness and pain in them. He could be cheerful and deal with such matters due to his real sense of the victory of the gospel in an evil world. John's aim has always been to use every opportunity that came his way to further his vision of the gospel of Christ, the 'way of love' as he called it over and over again in his sermons. His office as canon of St. Paul's has always been used to further that purpose, and when the time comes for the historians to make their judgements on these matters, I believe he will be acknowledged among the very few who have had some success in our day in making the Christian gospel known and heard in a work-a-day world. At a time when the church has very largely retreated into a narcissistic concern with its own self and its own doings, he has always been concerned to proclaim Christ's way of love to and for the world. In this he is surely right.

2 MAN AND SOCIETY

Thomas Corbishley

The work of Christian Action, as its name implies, is primarily concerned with activity of one sort or another. But perhaps it is no bad thing if we look at the underlying philosophical basis of such activities. If this chapter seems a little academic and remote, it does nevertheless seem to provide a contribution towards what we may call the philosophy of Christian Action.

The very title of this chapter calls for some comment. Indeed an analysis of its meaning is the best way to open up our whole subject. For it implies that there is some sort of distinction between man in his individuality and man as a member of a community. It is the whole point of this chapter that there is not a disjunction between these two. On the contrary, man can be himself fully and perfectly only in so far as he is (and is conscious of being) organically, psychologically and spiritually linked with and integrated into a larger whole to which he makes his contribution and thereby enriches not merely the group to which he belongs but himself as a member of that group and in his own right.

It is arguable that the failure to appreciate this two-sided, almost paradoxical truth lies at the root of most of the major misunderstandings which divide mankind. Take the first and most obvious example – the cold war between the communist bloc and what is called the capitalist world. As a rough generalization it is fair to say that each side in this confrontation emphasizes one aspect of the whole truth. The communist, ideally and ideologically, thinks primarily in terms of the general good, overriding and overruling the individual's ambitions and personal aspirations. The capitalist thinks in terms of the individual's achievements, the success of private enterprise, the freedom of men and women to be themselves . . . It is true that both theories recognize (certainly in theory and to some extent in practice) the validity of the opposite conception. Thus whilst the capitalist argues that his form of economic growth is the best for the country as a whole, the Marxist bases his appeal to the masses on the hope that communism will mean a better life for those who work to promote it.

So too within Christendom, the division between Protestantism and Catholicism can be seen as largely a struggle between those with an individualistic view of religion and those who think of religion primarily in terms of its social, organic and institutional nature, emphasizing authority as against freedom of conscience, structure as against charism, law as against inspiration. The ecumenical movement should be seen therefore as concerned with these deeper issues and not primarily with questions of dogma, liturgical practice or any of the forms of religious observance.

We begin then by recognizing that man is indeed an individual. I am I and not another, with this particular collection of chromosomes, occupying this particular spot in the whole space-time continuum, with my own heredity, environment, experience, education – all that has gone to the production of my temperament, my peculiar reaction to a given situation; in a word, all that makes me *me*. In an important and not unworthy sense, I am the centre of the universe, in that all the sensations, inferences, judgements, moral decisions and emotional reactions which give meaning and purpose to my life are mine and nobody else's. The whole evolutionary process, from the first moment of time until this present instant, has gone to the making of me, in all my uniqueness. The existentialist approach to the meaning of life is in its fundamental doctrine profoundly significant.

But then, I reflect, what *I* am saying about myself is what every single human being on the face of the earth has said in the past about himself or is saying now in precisely the same sort of way. Although this individual that I am is utterly unique, *my* uniqueness is in some mysterious, indescribable way shared by everybody. The very term 'ego' which lies at the root of the attitude of mind we call egotism is appropriated by every single conscious human entity. The title which is most completely individualistic, which distinguishes me from anybody and everybody else, is at the same time one which applies to them all as well. Similarly if, as I claim with justice, I have a right to be myself, to make my own decisions, to exercise a personal responsibility, this again can be true only if it is true of all those other centres of rights, responsibilities and decision-making capabilities.

Moreover, experience of life gradually brings me to the realization that I am moulded to a very great extent not by cold intellectual reactions to a mathematical system but by my response to other beings like myself. It is not merely that I draw my very existence from two other individuals, that in my formative years I am trained, educated and indoctrinated by others; at a much deeper level, it is true to say that I exist fully in the degree to which I am at once an appeal and a response to others. Technically speaking, I can go on living in splendid isolation. With the jolly miller I can sing:

> I care for nobody, no not I,
> If nobody cares for me.

But I know that in that case I am merely whistling in the dark. Even the drop-out from society seeks the company of like-minded fellows. For as Aristotle said all those centuries ago, the man without friends is either a wild beast or a god. For what is called self-consciousness is never simply *self*-consciousness. I become conscious of myself only in and through consciousness of realities other than myself. I am for example conscious of the fact that I am at this moment sitting at my typewriter, composing this chapter. What I call my self-consciousness is a consciousness of my fingers hitting the keys, my ears hearing the rattle of the typeface against the paper, awareness of the various objects on my desk. If I stop typing in order to think out the next paragraph, my thinking is in a strange way related to ideas which are somehow outside me, over against me, even whilst I appropriate them to myself, making them my own. If my mind really did become a complete blank, if I stopped being aware of the chair in which I am sitting, if I closed my eyes to all sights and so on, I should become not more but less conscious of myself.

This is at the superficial level. But at the deeper level of personal development, how true it is to say

Without the other, an other who takes account of me and for whom my free response means something, I do not exist. I can be myself only in your presence. But if I need you in order to be myself, you likewise need me. Each of us holds his 'personhood' as a gift from the other, so that to betray the other is always to betray oneself. As persons, we are each of us responsible to and for the other, and only in the mutual fulfilment of this responsibility do we secure for ourselves a place in the real.

Building the Human 82/3

It is this primordial psychological truth which is at the basis of the idea that man is *zoon politikon*, not simply a 'political' animal, but a being whose nature demands that he shall live in the *polis*, in a society of likeminded, free, responsible fellows, sharing the same ideals, hopes, aspirations and achievements. In a famous passage, Thomas Hobbes described the human condition without the organization of the state:

> no arts; no society; and which is worst of all, continual fear and danger of violent death; and the life of man solitary, poor, nasty, brutish and short.

True as it undoubtedly is that (as a matter of history) men first drew together for mutual protection against external enemies, what keeps them together is the recognition of the many positive advantages to be gained from association, advantages which of course include various material benefits, but reach far beyond these to the whole sphere of man's complete psychological and spiritual development. What we call civilization is much more than the absence of barbarism. It includes the whole range of man's social, philosophical, aesthetic, political, moral and religious constructs, which provide the larger framework within which his more localized and more individual experiences are protected and nourished.

Within that larger framework, for example, we pursue our own limited interests, we drink at our local pub, we go to the local cinema to watch a film which may have been produced in Hollywood six thousand miles away, we watch on our television screens the activities of men on the moon a quarter of a million miles away, we fall in love, marry, bring up a family, buy toys for the children, mow the lawn, borrow books from the library, give parties, go to church and eventually, of course, get buried . . . This we feel is our life, as indeed it is. But the point is that it is supported by a vast network of interrelated activities which enable me not merely to exist, to grow, but specifically *to be myself*. What I am in fact doing – and I remind myself that 'I' refers not just to this particular individual that 'I' am but to *every member of the community to which I belong* – is to help to build a world in which individuals become themselves; they become themselves in building that world.

We are faced with another example of the age-old problem about the hen and the egg. Community clearly cannot exist without its constituent individuals; equally the individuals cannot be themselves without the community. And like so many problems that have no clear-cut logical solution, *solvitur ambulando*. In other words the individual has to sink himself in the building of the community; equally, the community can realize its own purpose only in realizing the perfection of the individual: that is, his happiness, physical well-being, intellectual growth, and his moral and spiritual fulfilment. The world of communion is the only world which can provide a true habitat for man, wherein through communion he can be himself, himself precisely because no longer an isolated individual. 'Only communion at once preserves the miracle of originality that is the person, while at the same time healing the isolation that became his lot when self-consciousness first wrenched him from the mothering embrace of Nature.'

And here it would seem we encounter the real moral and spiritual problem lying behind all man's efforts to achieve harmony, both within himself and within the community of which he is a constituent element. Man's self-centredness needs to be transcended if he is to arrive at that fulfilment of himself-in-community which, as the foregoing analysis would suggest, is the only way to true human completeness. Is it possible to speculate that what we call original sin is precisely this inability to see one's individual selfhood in the context of the larger community? The metaphysical truth to which we referred earlier, that there is a valid sense in which man is the centre of the universe, has to be balanced by an appreciation of the fact that what is true of me is true of every intelligence that exists. To put it another way: the purely rational consideration is inadequate as a presentation of the whole truth. It must be inspired and warmed by those moral considerations which are not less truly rooted in the nature of things.

There are three specific problems I should now like to try to deal with in the light of what has already been said – the relation of man to a world society, the role of the individual in the church, and the interconnexion of freedom and authority.

First, then, a world society. If there is one lesson to be learnt from history it is surely that human progress has been a movement parallel to the enlarging political vision of men. It was only after the mosaic of scattered elements in Attica had formed an association to set up a common political centre that the great age of

Athenian culture began. But the Greek conception of humanity was marred by a failure to see beyond the narrow limits imposed by a very localized patriotism, to say nothing of the arrogant distinction between Greek and barbarian and the even worse failing which denied elementary political rights to the slave population on which much of their material prosperity depended. It was under the impetus of Alexander's conquests that men first began to glimpse the truth of the statement that art knows no frontiers. For all its many and glaring defects, medieval society did at least recognize a certain internationalism of the mind so that the scholars and the artists were much more the products of a universal culture than the boast of this or that country.

For too long the rise of the national spirit checked to some extent the practical expression of this ideal until in modern times the publication of (for example) scientific discoveries has been censored in the interests of national security, and national pride is somehow bound up with the accumulation and retention of artistic treasures in this or that country. Yet all the time the pressure of necessity is compelling nations which are politically estranged one from another to co-operate in various fields where a universal convention is seen to be advisable for the sake of individual national interests. Economic developments are already making a significant contribution to closer co-operation across national frontiers and even across the Iron Curtain. An American observer remarked recently that 'multinational corporations . . . may be the hoped-for force that will ultimately provide a means of unifying and reconciling the interests of mankind'. The purely negative argument that is based on the common threat hanging over the globe may provide yet another incentive for men to recognize the simple truth that man's best interests at every level are best served by a practical acceptance of the basic Christian teaching about the brotherhood of man under the fatherhood of God. It is a sardonic commentary on the ways of the human heart that, just as not a few people find themselves praying only when they are faced with some extreme danger or threatened loss, so men as a whole can be compelled only by economic necessity or advantage to admit the validity of an underlying spiritual truth.

After this excursion into history, politics and economics, I want now to turn to another aspect of this question of man in society – man in ecclesiastical society, that is the church. At what we call the social level man needs the company of his fellows, needs them

22

because of his psychological make-up as well as his material requirements. In the same sort of way and for the same sort of reasons, he needs a church, a company of likeminded human beings who will support him even as he supports them in the taxing business of religious activity. I propose to look at this department of our general subject from two starting-points. First of all, recalling what the church is for, I should like to suggest how we should think of our contribution to that purpose, how the individual can contribute to the total achievement of the whole body. Correspondingly, I should then wish to ask about the responsibility of the church to the individual, how she can best ensure his fulfilment for which she in her turn exists.

Obviously this is no place for a wide-ranging ecclesiological survey. I want to concentrate on that aspect of the church's mission in the world which is relevant to the subject of this chapter. What I should like to do is to focus on the religious ideas which underlie much of what I have been saying. I began by recognizing the importance of the individual simply *qua* this particular human being. At a later stage I referred to the brotherhood of man with its correlative, the fatherhood of God. What the Christian believes is that, in the final analysis, what gives man his importance is the fact that he is, in a special sense, the object of God's *love*. Analogously to the way in which each child is uniquely precious to a parent, so we believe every member of the human family is loved in a unique and individual way by the Creator who is ultimately responsible for the existence of each and every one of us. I am entitled to accept this explanation of why I am kept in being, but only if I am prepared to see that the same explanation goes for everybody else. In other words, we have to try to see the whole web of human relations held together by the all-pervading creative love of God.

It is what we may call this metaphysical truth which underlies the two great commandments of the Law: thou shalt love the Lord thy God – and thy neighbour *as thyself*. It helps us, I believe, especially to appreciate this second commandment. Seeing my neighbour as standing in the same relationship to God as I do myself, I ought to be able to see that he has the same value that I have, the same significance, the same ultimate purpose. If I have the modesty to recognize that whatever my abilities may be, whatever I may have achieved in life, I am not literally a 'self-made man' – I could not have done any of this without the talents (of whatever sort) with which I was born – if I am prepared to admit that my ultimate value is God-given, then I can begin to see my fellow men in the same light. Whatever our differences of background, interest, attractiveness and so on, none of this *sub specie aeternitatis* is relevant. I may not like him one bit; but I can appreciate his ultimate worth, which is not less than mine because it has the same origin and the same end.

When people talk about religion being 'irrelevant', it is because they have failed to see that, at one level, this is really what religion is all about. I am ready to admit that religion – and not least the Christian version of it – does not have a very good record in this matter. Concentrating on the first commandment, it has all too often lost sight of the fact that the second commandment is, in effect, the way in which men are called upon to implement the first. But the many failures of Christian folk to live up to the demands of their faith in no way invalidates that faith and its claims. However I am not so much concerned to discuss the claims of religion as to point out that it is only some transcendental view of man which can justify the attitude of the thoroughgoing humanist. At the purely phenomenal, empirical level there seems to be no particular reason why I should have any special regard for a starving peasant in India or a Vietnamese villager caught in the crossfire of warring powers. But once we have come to see that human worth is the manifestation of divine power, then God's presence among men becomes the very ground of our instinctive response to man's need. And this, as I see it, is what the church really exists for. Through its institutions it embodies God's presence in our midst, as the root and life-giving sap of our personal union one with another. 'Religion is the institutional basis of universal communion.' You may well be inclined to say that this is not how religion is often presented; to which I can only reply that it is up to the members of the church to make that presentation an abiding reality.

Which brings me to the other of my two starting-points, the responsibility of the church for the individual. And here we are faced with a two-sided problem. On the one hand, it must ever be borne in mind that the church – I mean of course the church as institution, as opposed to the church as people of God – is a means, not an end in itself. It exists simply to promote the general well-being of the individuals that are its members. 'The church was made for man, not man for the church.' On the other hand, since the individual's responsibility is to serve his fellow men and so to serve God, this will inevitably involve some limitation of individual initiative. If the church exists for the good of all its members – if, in other words, the church is to be able to serve everybody – this will mean some form of organization, some form of machinery, some structure to ensure the pooling of resources which will make it possible for individual contributions to be most effectively deployed to a common end.

Now it is in the nature of things that institutions, because they tend to be concerned with the general rather than the particular, have about them a certain impersonal quality. To what extent can I honestly believe that the institutional church is nevertheless promoting the good of the individual? Well, I suppose, in two main ways. In the first place, however intelligent and disinterested I may believe myself to be, a decent modesty will suggest that I am likely to make a more effective contribution to the general good if I insert myself into an institutional framework which will help me, as this individual with the limited resources I possess, to enlarge my sphere of influence and thereby to approximate more to the universality of service which ideally is my vocation. The very discipline of collaboration is often a strengthening and enriching experience. Secondly, of course, I can make my contribution precisely by helping to ensure that the institution, the structure, remains as flexible as possible, that it does not harden into an iron rule which is incapable of accommodating itself to the individual case.

To come then to the third problem I proposed to discuss, the relation of freedom to authority: what I should like to say is summed up in a sentence from the American political philosopher, Hannah Arendt: 'Authority implies an obedience in which men retain their freedom'. Since freedom is one of the two essential ways in which man resembles his Creator, it is as constitutive of his very being as much as his rationality. Any abuse of his freedom, any denial of it, is contrary to the very nature of things. From time to time the *exercise* of such freedom may need to be limited, not only for the general good but also for the benefit even of the individual concerned. We have a whole range of laws – the simplest example is the speed limit – which are designed to enable human beings to live together in safety, harmony and fruitful collaboration. What Rahner calls the 'temporary pedagogical limitation of freedom' is only justified if it really leads to a greater liberation of the personality. A final quotation from the same source may serve to sum up most of what I have been trying to say:

The purpose of the State can only be the preservation of human freedom. The State is a necessary consequence of the growth and complexification of human society. It does not give man his rights; it exists rather for their preservation.

Much of the foregoing analysis may seem too remote from the day-to-day activities of Christian Action to be genuinely relevant. Moreover, it is obvious that the immediate inspiration of many of the activities of its members springs from a sense of compassion at the sight of human suffering, indignation at injustice, or a simple desire to improve the human lot. Many perhaps will need nothing further. Yet it remains true that, at least from time to time, it is both reasonable and helpful that we should stop and ask ourselves the sort of questions about the nature of man, his purpose in life, his claims, his responsibilities, which do not get asked with sufficient frequency or sufficient persistence; we are too busy being busy. We need to see beyond the immediate task – concern for injustice in South Africa, efforts to house the homeless, to care for the drop-out – to the all-pervading truth that the objects of our compassion have this claim upon us precisely because they are at the same level of importance as ourselves.

Certainly we need all the expertise, the technical skill, the capacity for sheer hard work which will make that work effective. In many ways what the members of Christian Action are doing is a job like any other job. If it means political involvement, they will need the sort of political awareness which will rescue them from naïvety. If it means social action of any kind, they will need to co-operate with and turn to existing institutions for help. What makes Christian Action *Christian* action is precisely the consciousness that where human beings – any human beings – are involved, we are faced with men and women who are in the deepest sense of the words brothers and sisters, not just beneficiaries of our compassion. They are at least that; but they are so much more.

3 MAN AND GOD

Edward Carpenter

'Words are the wise man's counters, he does not reckon by them but they are the money of fools.'

This is a typical aphorism of the great English philosopher Thomas Hobbes, both in its truth and dangerous half-truth. Yet his is no solitary voice. In our own day the linguistic analysts have forcefully reminded us of the need to know what we mean when we use words too cavalierly and base arguments upon them. They can cloud rather than illumine our thinking.

Language, however, cannot be confined to logical statements. Words 'operate' – they move us at different levels of experience. When Wordsworth writes of 'yon solitary highland lass' and exhorts us to 'listen for the vale profound is overflowing with the sound' he is saying something more than that someone is singing, and this 'more' can only be conveyed by subtle suggestion and an evocative use of language.

I begin with these seemingly remote reflections because I believe that the designation 'Christian Action' is itself deeply revealing, both in respect of the mood prevailing in the immediate post-war years and in providing a clue to the history of this dynamic movement particularly in its early days.

When the engines of war finally ground to a halt in 1945 and the nuclear bombs (not we hope for future use) were put back into the armoury of weapons, western Europe began to weave again the fabric of some civilized pattern of collective life. Yet there was, in spite of Britain's 'finest hour', a sense of shame in some circles that humanity could have engaged in such a holocaust of mutual slaughter. The expenditure of blood and treasure on so mammoth a scale, with its wastage of human life before that life had realized its fullest potential, brought with it a feeling of desperate need to redeem the years that the locusts had so wantonly devoured. Nor could Christians ignore the fact, nor ought they, that Nazism was brought to birth not in a country which had never known Christian faith but in one which cradled the Protestant Reformation and where the gospel had been preached and taken seriously for centuries. No subtle sophistry seemed then, or seems now, adequate to account for so gigantic a perversion. Certainly we thank God for such heroic figures as Pastor Niemöller and Dietrich Bonhoeffer, but the mystery of so incredible a phenomenon as Nazism remains.

So a war-weary generation asked: was it not time that the Christian turned away from works of destruction, necessary though many thought these works to be, in order to introduce into society and the life of nations a new solvent in the form of an active and truly Christian presence. In Britain William Temple prepared the way by quickening the conscience of responsible Christians to apply their faith to the collective as well as the individual life. Only by so doing could the past be atoned for and the crippling frustration of the agonizing years of conflict be removed. To many it was a case of 'he that doeth the will shall know of the doctrine'. The impatience to which Dick Sheppard called the attention of an earlier generation now took on a more concentrated social and less ecclesiastical preoccupation. It was a time to be up and doing. Christian Action directed itself to this mood. The very destructiveness of a world war, its primitive character linked to a high technology, the immediate confrontation with death – these had their usual effect, as in the first world war, of making ecclesiastical pretensions appear not so much absurd as irrelevant. 'Great and mean meet massed in death', war is no respecter of persons, it is the great leveller, and its long term effect adds a further momentum to the weakening process which minimizes absolute religious claims. Of course theological scholarship had been quietly preparing the way for such a climate of change. I recall numerous conversations with men from the forces in 1945 who found it difficult, in good faith, to dot the i's and cross the t's, putting their hands on their hearts and declaring that they really believed all the articles of the Christian faith. Yet they wanted to profess and call themselves Christians and to act accordingly.

There is nothing particularly novel in this. A concealed scepticism has accompanied Christianity across the centuries. Even in ages of faith, despite tremendous conditioning pressures, some men reflecting upon experience always find it difficult to reconcile public testimony and private conviction. The war years added to their number. It was not for a moment that they wished to renounce Christian faith, or felt themselves to be agnostic to the point of unbelief; rather they preferred to put the emphasis on practical action, on doing something in a world desperately needing the infusion of a power which could reconcile, which could build up the waste places and in doing this point the way ahead. This spirit, they believed, had been exemplified in Jesus. Detailed analysis of the tenets of Christian faith, so they unconsciously reasoned or more probably felt in their bones, might be right when one's primary concern is with truth statements in religion. But with a Europe half in ruins, with Belsen and its like a running sore, an unparalleled horror, and with Nagasaki and Hiroshima a charnel house, the unfortunate being the few who survived – the time was not yet. Was it not in the sphere of practice that we shall 'see salvation': and did not the gospel right at its heart enshrine the Dominical injunction 'Not everyone that saith unto me Lord, Lord, shall enter into the Kingdom of heaven but he that doeth the will of my father which is in heaven'? Cannot all Christians unite in actively promoting human brotherhood, removing the causes of war, and opposing the prevailing evil or depravity?

This emphasis on the practical, on involvement, the reluctance to engage too deeply in theological introspection, these were also in line with the implications of contemporary philosophical speculation.

If the logical positivists are right (only relatively), then to raise questions of ultimate meaning in human life as ontologically grounded is to pursue a will-o'-the-wisp, elusive, self-defeating, indeed a high human presumption. Those who found this too arid a view but were prepared reluctantly to accept its basic assumptions turned to existentialism as a more personal philosophy. In such as Jean Paul Sartre, existentialism became a heroic attitude against the background of universal agnosticism and unrelieved gloom. Yet paradoxically though life may be a sorry joke without even a cosmic joker to get a kick out of it, this need not prevent men – Promethean man, world-defying man – from making his own values as he goes along and through commitment to them authenticating himself until, head bloody but unbowed, the universe pulverizes him into nothingness.

29

Let me make myself clear. I am not suggesting that Christian Action recruited itself from Christian *manqués*, intellectual agnostics who found their integrity by living out an existentialist faith drawing its moral inspiration from Jesus. Not for a moment. What I am saying is, if I may be excused quoting the now hackneyed words of John Donne, that 'no man is an island'. He cannot be indifferent to what is going on around him. When an intellectual mood becomes prevalent and is hostile to traditional beliefs, many are the people who react, without necessarily any conscious act of will, by putting the emphasis where they believe a cherished conviction to be less vulnerable. We all do it. It is not that we accept current criticisms hook, line and sinker, or indeed have read them or would understand some of them if we did; rather that we are predisposed against exposing ourselves at points which are too sensitive. The general effect of existentialism, whether that existentialism was near to Christianity or far removed from it, was to place the emphasis on commitment to action, on definitive decision-making. A man becomes himself by his individual response to the critical situations which life imposes upon him. To dither and to do nothing, to become a victim of circumstances, is to diminish as a person. On the contrary, to be up and doing, to be active about one's own (and others') predicament rather than nihilistically succumb to it, this 'like they glory Titan is to be . . . Empire and Victory'.

This may seem a surprisingly positive conclusion to draw from the existentialist premiss. Would it not be more appropriate for Sartre to suppose that the frame isn't really worth the candle, that there isn't much point in doing anything. But it does not work out this way any more than the doctrinaire Marxist, believing that his utopia will as surely emerge as day follows night, waits passively and supinely for its coming. This is certainly not the way he sees it. Indeed Sartre has a highly developed social conscience, as he consistently displays and on so many occasions. Commitment to the exigencies of practical living is of the essence of his 'gospel' and of his appeal. Whereas Thomas Hardy mildly, indeed with aesthetic grace, inveighs against his President of the Immortals, Sartre is not so respectful and his defiance leads to a social role. Tess in his eyes is to be blamed for acquiescence, for allowing herself to become a puppet on a string. Her psychological reaction is wrong. Equally Angel Clare would have done better to make his own values rather than destroy his own life and hers by inability to release himself from the shackles of conventional moral norms. If he could not change society at least he could change his reaction to that society.

I hope I have not laboured the point, but it is important to see the genesis of Christian Action (and some of its continuing problems) against the background of the varying moods of the forties – moods which united in a call to action of a kind with a different character and motivation from that which had obtained during the devastating years of war. For relatively young men, fed up with violence and anxious to build bridges instead of knocking them down and concerned to make Christian faith (however they understood it) a reality in the social, economic and political life of their neighbourhood and nation, Christian Action seemed the answer. To such John Collins became a symbol embodying this hope and his movement the expression of their collective will. He had himself become caught up in the war machine as a chaplain; he had behind him a not inconsiderable academic achievement and might have continued to pursue this way as a profession. His invasion of the citadels of power and decision-making had more than a personal significance. To a generation who believed (in the main and paradoxically) that the war must be fought and won but constituted a collective shame, Christian Action seemed to meet, at least for some, their spiritual and moral demands.

However, the very designation 'Christian Action', apart from its emotional overtones, is ambiguous and carries at least two meanings along with it.

It can mean action which flows directly from a Christian position and which ought as such to constrain the individual conscience. It can also mean action which any man of goodwill and high principles ought to engage in but which the Christian, because of his beliefs, finds particularly compelling. Let me illustrate.

According to the first, it would be reasonable for a pacifist to affirm that pacifism was for him a necessary expression of the theology of the cross and only within this context does it become for him a valid personal commitment. He might, from his point of view, go on to say that if he wishes to commend pacifism as a moral obligation he would feel it necessary first to commend the Christian faith as a true statement of man's existential predicament. This would not rule out his admitting that other people might hold pacifist convictions on different grounds, though these would not carry the same weight with him.

31

This view, it will be noticed, claims that there is something *sui generis* in Christian faith (and I am not in this paper concerned with other faiths) which illuminates the moral consciousness and gives it a set of values which can be translated into specific action. The authentication of this claim is both difficult and complex, and many Christians would not find it easy of acceptance particularly when it relates to the life of society as a whole. Indeed some theologians have claimed – very improperly in my opinion – that Christian principles, relevant in relation to family and friends, have no place in the policy of states. However if we take a leaf out of Plato's book, who when seeking to define justice preferred to 'blow it up' in terms of the just society, we may be able to take a more long term view. Here I believe it to be true that in a society where for some centuries Christian faith has been preached and practised, if only fitfully, the conscience will register different behaviour patterns from those in a society committed, shall we say, to Stoicism or Buddhism. Priorities would be different; personal relations would have a different 'feel' about them; attitudes to collective goals would not develop the same trust. I am not arguing here that one is more developed than the other; simply that there would be a difference. Christianity seems to place a unique emphasis on the particularity of the individual person; history is seen as a real dimension, demanding commitment to rather than escape from it. Over the centuries such attitudes undoubtedly affect law and government behaviour patterns generally.

When, however, we turn from considering Christianity in a wider context to its introduction into immediate situations the view which holds that there are specifically Christian behaviour patterns runs into a practical difficulty, since it must be confessed that there is no general consensus amongst equally intelligent Christians as to what these patterns are. Let me illustrate from my own experience.

I have always regarded capital punishment as an impiety which outrages and does violence to specifically Christian insights. It seems to me *inter alia* to deny the Christian doctrine of redemption, to write off the significance of the time world and to usurp a divine prerogative in the absolute judgement in which it engages. To me this is transparently clear, so much so that I regard every judicial execution as saying publicly, 'The Christian faith is not true'. (This does not mean, of course, that there are not other and cogent reasons to deplore capital punishment.) However, in stumping the country on behalf of the campaign for its abolition I soon found that my view was by no means acceptable to a large number of Christians. Indeed it was often in these circles that the desire to retain it seemed strongest, so much so that to further the cause it was often wiser to avoid references to Christian faith. As to the cause of abolition humanists in general proved far more sympathetic and suggestive.

The fact is that on a large number of great moral issues, individual and collective, none of them trivial, the Christian conscience is divided: euthanasia, artificial insemination and genetic control; war in general, the nuclear bomb in particular; factory farming, the way in which man should discharge his stewardship of God's creation – the list could be almost endlessly prolonged. In respect of these there is no unanimity of view. Perhaps this will occasion no surprise, but it needs to be reiterated that none of these questions is trivial or unimportant; they pose questions as to the nature of the human person, how society ought to deal with him, and he with himself.

Two brief observations as to this situation may be offered.

Some will see it as a clear recognition that most moral judgements are existential and personal: they arise out of the individual's unique life and experience. What matters is that he authenticates himself.

Others will, perhaps, take comfort from the fact that over a long period of years consensus moral judgements do emerge – for example in this country, slavery – and this justifies the initial and seemingly unsuccessful efforts to commend them. As in aesthetic evaluations time is the final arbiter; and given this, the Christian conscience registers itself unequivocally.

Two other escape routes have been adopted to deal with this very real dilemma. For example, William Temple eirenically asserted during the last war that God had placed the constraint of pacifism on a small minority of Christians in order that the ethics of God's perfect kingdom should still be witnessed to in a world of violence. The majority of Christians, in the meantime, must get on with winning the war. This is indeed a difficult position to maintain, though it is testimony to his charity.

The other escape route is for a majority of official pronouncements to be couched in terms of general principles, leaving it to the individual person to work out what these principles mean in practice. Understandably, if not always fairly, this expedient provokes the somewhat cynical comment that it is this very generality which leads to many such pronouncements being platitudinous and lacking in any effective cutting edge. Incidentally it is the reversal of this policy which makes recent pronouncements issued by the World Council of Churches unpopular in the west. The fact is that few people within the congregation of Christian people are prepared to dispute principles; it is the application of them into particular situations which leads to difficulty and proves divisive. Thus Archbishop Fisher wrote to Canon Collins way back in April 1948, in connexion with a publication preparatory to a meeting in the Albert Hall:

> I have a further difficulty about all the paragraphs. They might be held to suggest that in every particular situation there is (one) particular application of Christian principles upon which all Christians ought to unite. It is a mere fact that at many practical points Christians equally sincere and equally starting from Christian premises may reach different judgements as to the right cause of action. I think it is truer and more realistic if it can be suggested somewhere that each (*sic*) of the people is responsible to form his judgement of Christian principles to the best of his ability.

No one can dispute at the factual level the accuracy of the Archbishop's words. To profess a common principle such as respect for the integrity of the human person can and does lead to a bewildering variety of attitudes in its application. Those responsible for the Inquisition in Spain managed to convince themselves that death by burning, taking a long view, was in the final interests of the condemned. Indeed even where the church has endeavoured to lay down practical absolutes as in the indissolubility of marriage this has been subject to revision and adjustment in practice. Many theologians would thus maintain that practical answers to specifically personal problems cannot be deduced from Christian doctrine by any logical inference. In the ordinary everyday world Christians disagree amongst themselves as to what ought to be done, as do secularists and humanists. It is because of this that law-making is so difficult an exercise since it must deal in universals and take some account of a general consensus opinion. For this reason many maintain that it must be kept at a minimum.

So we turn, more briefly, to the second understanding of the term Christian Action. It is that since there is such variety, Christian faith must be understood not as pointing to behaviour patterns deeply embedded in its own insights but as giving its imprimatur to general principles upon which all men of goodwill ought to be able to agree – that is without rooting such principles in any ontological or transcendental claims. What faith does is to give an extra fillip to the will thus convincing the believer that what he is fighting for has behind it that Providence which makes all things work together for good. It braces him to action and encourages him to keep going when things are against him in the same way as Hegelian dialectic encourages the Marxist and sustains his motivation.

So we have a built-in dilemma which no sophistry can entirely remove. It can be simply expressed, at the risk of repetition. Devotion to common principles does not necessarily mean devotion to common action. Yet merely to affirm principles unless they can be so translated (and this translation makes a difference) would serve only to frustrate and achieve little. Indeed in the light of what we have suggested earlier about commitment it could be stultifying. Yet there is something odd about commitment, to action arising out of common principles, which yet leads to a number of irreconcilable patterns of behaviour in those areas where it is difficult for them to co-exist. Nor is it less of an oddity when it is explained that this 'pluralism' is due to the infinite variety of humankind and the near infinite variety of situations in which this humankind finds itself. Alas! Untold suffering can result while these different attitudes jostle and compete with each other waiting some final resolution.

Some will say that we must accept this situation as inevitably bound up with our human predicament. Though we are right to believe that certain political, social and economic systems are nearer to Christian insights than some others (which means we must bear our own responsibility and act accordingly) we must not expect all good Christian men to see things our way. Such a recognition need not blunt the cutting edge of our Christian witness; but it will demand of us charity and humility. Neither the Pope with his pronouncements on contraception nor myself with my views on capital punishment is infallible. No policy is wholly in accord with Christian insights. The intention of the Christian is to lift personal relations into a higher dimension of mutual and sacrificial self-giving. At one level this will mean the search for justice, at another the realization of love. It also means that mankind must act responsibly and with compassion in its stewardship of God's creation, not least to the animals.

It is in this complex, ambiguous and mixed social scene that I believe Christian Action has a particular and necessary role to discharge – and that on the whole it has discharged it well and with distinction. Placing the priority on action in Christian discipleship is not simply a subjective demand, a means of overcoming the inhibitions of the individual believer, though it may have this effect. The object of the exercise is to get things done which ought to be done in the interest of society, and in the process to move a little nearer to a just or Christian order – that is an order shaped so as to make it more easy to realize Christian and humane values in so far as these values can be freely achieved and freely opted for. It would, therefore, be impracticable to impose upon society behaviour patterns opposed by the overwhelming mass of its members, though it might be proper for a minority either to withdraw its support or claim to authenticate its own corporate existence in so far as this did not prevent other people from authenticating theirs. In the increasingly pluralist societies of today the latter situation will more frequently occur.

Christian Action was born not by reflection in the study on the nature of politics, but in vision and compassion, kindled into life through the harsh realities of the social and political scene.

To make an effective impact it was essential that the membership should consist of likeminded people. *Within* a group there is not much point in Christians being active if they are all pulling contrary ways. Nor does it work in practice for a relatively small organization to break itself down into smaller units each with its own preoccupations. By so doing resources are dissipated and human energy wasted. No clear image is built up. It is perhaps significant in this context that Christian Action has on the whole attracted a left wing membership. This was certainly not due to any positive intention on the part of John Collins. Indeed quite the reverse. Such men as Lord Halifax were prominent in the beginning, and other right wing personnel were cherished rather than rejected, as efforts were made to keep a party political balance. But the simple fact is that the causes which Christian Action espoused and which commanded its main energies were such as tended to engage the interest of those on the left or radical ends of the political spectrum. Right wing personnel (there were exceptions of course) tended to become embarrassed, and rather than dragging their feet preferred to fold up their tents like the Arabs and silently steal away. I have not done the necessary homework but I should be interested to know how many of those who let their membership lapse or who formally resigned were left, centre or right of centre. I suspect the last by a vast majority. Their departure, and I can say this without making any judgement on them, was essential to a frontal attack on certain social ills. There needed to be cohesion and a unifying sense of purpose at the level of what is thought necessary to be done. Also needed was the spirit of a crusade. It is for this reason that such a group cannot hope to express the whole mind of the Christian community, since if it casts its net too widely it will have little thrust and make no significant impact.

This meant establishing a set of priorities springing out of contemporary and real issues; issues, that is, where it was felt Christian insights *were* involved, whether in the prompting of judgement or the sustaining of passion. In establishing these priorities Christian Action proved, I think, to be right. Most people associate it pre-eminently with race relations, and in this they are not far from the truth. The race issue has commanded most of its attention and no one can deny that it is a major, if not *the* major issue of our times. By bending its efforts this way, though this has meant excluding other interests, Christian Action has been wise. In the years immediately after the war racial equality and opposition to apartheid were not popular causes to espouse, and many were the people who tended to drag their feet and suspend judgement. Hence the need for a group which was prepared as I like to put it to be responsibly irresponsible, and this in a double way: irresponsible in that there were situations to which it must chance its arm; irresponsible also in that it has no delegated membership to embarrass or come to terms with.

Many years ago now Archbishop Davidson was asked to condemn the wretched conditions of Chinese labour in the mines of the Transvaal after the South African war. He felt uncertain as to the precise facts, and annoyed Bishop Gore greatly by the use of such words as 'I feel that if indeed the necessity [of the camps] be real it is one of the most regrettable necessities that has ever arisen in the history of our colonial government'. Randall Davidson wanted to know all the facts to satisfy himself in every jot and tittle before he made a definitive pronouncement in public or approached the Government direct. This is understandable in an archbishop. The fact is, however, that a developing situation seldom makes this possible, and when it does become possible it is usually too late. I can remember well how in the 'fifties a few of us – John Fletcher I remember in particular – met with John Collins in 2 Amen Court in a small Race Relations group. Our concern was with South Africa. At that time many ecclesiastics were bending over backwards to find a justification for apartheid and seeking a rationale, if not for an outright defence, at least for not opposing it overmuch. The group was accused of irresponsibility, passing judgement without knowing all the facts, rocking the boat, etc. Nowadays, however, most of what the group then said is a commonplace, and has become an established position among nearly all churches. Perhaps it is a tribute *inter alia* to Christian Action that opinion has in the United Kingdom swung round (albeit tardily) to see things this way. Better late than never. Certainly it is a very small mind which takes offence when a minority and non-respectable view is taken over by more orthodox and hierarchical institutions. Surely this was the object of the exercise, and what one ought to hope would happen. We must expect traditional and long established bodies to be difficult to move: the odd thing is that when they do finally move they can move rapidly. But they would not do so without persistent and uncomfortable prodding. Here Christian Action has served well. I have already used the phrase 'chancing one's arm'. To be prepared to do just this demands humility – one may prove to be wrong – but it is on occasions essential. I am not for a single moment encouraging eccentric judgements which have no factual or informational foundation: what I am maintaining is that there are situations when to wait for certitude in exposing an evil is to miss an opportunity for halting the progress of that evil. The condition for a majority opinion to register itself is often for a minority to incur odium. There is no disgrace (though politicians all too often seem to think there is) in admitting that one is wrong. An individual with any sensitivity often finds himself in this position.

For this reason I think it was probably a mistake for Christian Action to seek any official representation on its inner councils, and that Archbishop Fisher was probably right in finally withholding it. A group should not seek any official recognition unless it is willing to be geared down to the pace of the slowest vessel in the convoy or is prepared to land itself in tremendous internal difficulties. I remember a prominent bishop, in respect of an equally prominent public issue, counselling the church to go slow. I could not refrain from remarking that this seemed like urging a tortoise to lose speed. This was a lesson, however, which Christian Action learned the hard way in its early years and only after much heart searching. It is interesting to note here that, in the very early days of Christian Action, the Archbishop offered John Collins the secretaryship of the British Council of Churches, but this, John knew instinctively, would take him too far into the establishment and would make it impossible for him to build up the kind of 'gadfly' movement that he envisaged, so he unhesitatingly refused the offer.

Nevertheless John Collins, like many radical social prophets, was far more orthodox in his theological than in his political opinions. The thought of standing over against the church was far less palatable to him than standing over against the state. He wanted the church to come in on, and to approve what Christian Action was doing. Indeed he saw it as a handmaid of the church. The presence on the platform of such a high churchman as Lord Halifax and a sprinkling of bishops seemed right. But official representation can be an embarrassment all round. If it is to have any reality there must be constant reference back, a sustained desire to put the brake on and to encourage enunciation of principles rather than to espouse concrete political action. Also the representative, no matter how much he may wish to be otherwise, tends to see himself as a kind of watchdog. It was no surprise therefore, when Armstrong, the Archbishop's nominee on the Council, left it in November 1954, that the Archbishop of Canterbury declined to appoint a successor, having written earlier to Canon Collins that it was better to keep Christian Action and himself free. This position he maintained, and in a letter dated November 29 he confessed: 'I had one little finger in your concern and no more'. It was indeed best for both parties that they should part, as John Collins himself later came to realize. Thus in connexion with a letter to *The Times* concerning the passive resistance by Indians and coloureds in South Africa the Canon wrote:

> I realize that this is a very much more 'tricky' matter than the one on Federation (and as a naughty freelance person, perhaps thought to be even irresponsible by some, I can become involved in 'tricky things'!) and therefore hesitate even to suggest that you might consider adding your signature. But I will be, nevertheless, foolhardy enough to overcome my hesitation and just to entertain the faintest little ray of hope that you might say 'yes'.

To this charmingly ingenuous letter the Archbishop replied:

> To put it bluntly I am afraid I should not dream of signing your letter to the *Times*.

There were not lacking those who *ab initio* sounded a note of alarm and advised the Archbishop to keep clear of any involvement with Christian Action. Prominent among its critics was the secretary of the Council of Foreign Relations, Herbert Waddams, whose clinical intelligence led him to offer frequent advice to Lambeth. In 1952 he was urging the Archbishop not to associate himself with a particular meeting, since among other objections consorting with Roman Catholics might prejudice reunion with the Orthodox Churches. Such counsel is significant since it admirably illustrates how an ecclesiastical interest, irrelevant to the point at issue, could condition a judgement.

So two mutually exclusive views developed – that Christian Action must be independent or it must be controlled by the official churches. In reply to a criticism which Waddams had drawn up, Alec Vidler in describing John Collins as 'one of my most intimate friends' added: 'the enterprises we have in mind are not official ecclesiastical ones like the British Council of Churches'. Armstrong himself recognized that it would not be helpful either for Christian Action to become another semi-official church organization or for it to develop too complex an organization. It became necessary, however, for Christian Action to make application (which the Archbishop against the advice of some of his counsellors supported) to be registered as a charity; and Canon Collins himself confessed ' . . . it is a disaster that we should have to formulate ourselves'. Alan Don, Dean of Westminster, a dour and charming Scotsman, admitted to being worried at the early progress of the movement. He had 'misgivings', he told the Archbishop, over the 'kind of activities which Christian Action proposes to sponsor' and added that it was 'in the highest degree desirable that Collins should be in close touch with the British Council of Churches in order to avoid the danger of his taking precipitate action'. Cripps, he complained, gave Christian Action 'Anglican respectability'.

In this respect the attitude of Bishop Bell of Chichester is interesting. His devotion and sacrificial concern to introduce political insights into the social, economic and political ordering of society is beyond dispute. Indeed in this area he was a giant, and it was therefore natural for him to preside over the inaugural meeting of Christian Action. His mind, however, tended to think in terms of official structures, particularly those of the British and World Council of Churches, of which he was a great protagonist. He had long kept in touch with John Collins but he thought it a pity that he should 'go on in his own individual way'. Armstrong with greater percipience, as already noted, took the view that it would be regrettable if efforts were made to secure that Christian Action became 'yet another formal Christian organization competing with the British Council of Churches'. John Collins himself, he said, accepted that it was not an 'official Christian organization'.

Geoffrey Fisher at first saw himself as steering a middle course. He attended some meetings, though he refused to go to the Albert Hall in December 1949, because he was under a 'bond' to the Archbishop of Cape Town 'to take no part in the desperately difficult South African problem beyond applauding what our Bishops there have done and are doing'. The Archbishop, partly under the influence of Bishop Bell, thought it was essential that Christian Action should keep in close touch with church bodies already at work in various fields, as for example the Council of Foreign Relations, all of which he assured John Collins would show 'entire willingness to co-operate'. But, fortunately, things did not work out this way. The fact that Christian Action was forced finally to go it alone undoubtedly gave it manœuvrability and encouraged campaign activities directed towards specialized objectives. For this reason many worthwhile causes have rightly lain completely outside its efforts. I remember Christian Action laying on a one-day conference concerning safety on the road. No cause deserves more support, for the criminality of some road users leads to countless deaths and untold suffering. I remember the conference well, for I chaired it. We spent an agreeable day, and if my memory serves me well almost the only publicity given to it was the observation of a Roman priest that he always said a short prayer to St. Christopher when crossing a London street. A happy day but nothing really came of it! This concern, this terribly necessary concern, was better left to others. Sometimes, it is true, Christian Action has taken up a cause, pioneered it a little way and then left it to others. But with a geographically dispersed membership, only certain causes were adequate to generate enthusiasm, and these reflected basically the deep social concerns of its founder John Collins. I cannot therefore forbear saying a few words in retrospect concerning his leadership.

'Leadership' has become almost a dirty word in the west, and no wonder. Millions of people all over the world have been led up the garden path to dreadful dooms by pathological, power-obsessed tyrants. Even leadership at a less demonic and more pedestrian level can all too easily sap the vitality of individual people. But this is bad leadership. In reverse informed and mature leadership can encourage pockets of leadership among others. A London based society with few local groups cannot really sustain itself without someone who comes to represent and embody the vision which inspires and the cause which demands sacrifice. John Collins served to bring a focal point to the aspirations and dedication of a large number of committed persons. The strength of his convictions and their outreach can be seen in that Defence and Aid (no official church body could ever have undertaken this demanding and necessary commitment), the campaigns for nuclear disarmament and against capital punishment are often thought of as activities of Christian Action itself. This is true only in the sense that the membership of the one flowed over to support the others under John Collins's unifying influence. The membership of Christian Action by and large trusted him, realizing that, within a general framework of principles and priorities which they approved *ad hoc* and on occasions, immediate judgements had to be made. Their confidence in him across the years was not misplaced. His steadfastness and courage are beyond praise.

PART TWO

CHRISTIAN ACTION
AND ACTION

1 THE BIRTH
OF A STRUGGLE

Trevor Huddleston

The most crucial and tormenting issue confronting those of us who were directly involved in the South African struggle in the 'forties and 'fifties can be very simply stated. It was the struggle to arouse the conscience of Britain and the world.

It is difficult to realize today, when South Africa and Rhodesia have become the focus of world opinion on the racist conflict; have become through their involvement in Angola and Namibia of major concern to east and west in the ideological conflict as well; have been for many years at the centre of dispute in the United Nations, that twenty years ago it was hard to arouse public sympathy for a crusade against 'apartheid'. Yet so it was.

In 1950 – the year in which Christian Action first moved into the field of race relations – I was still in Johannesburg and the spate of legislation restricting human rights was just begining to gather momentum. Ambrose Reeves was at the very start of his momentous episcopate. The Defiance Campaign had not begun. Michael Scott had been deported, but his lone, prophetic voice could not at that point in time carry very far. The fundamental reasons for his protest and for the courageous actions which expressed that protest were barely understood in South Africa itself – even less in Britain.

For at that time the Commonwealth was understood basically as an extension of the idea of Empire. The visit of King George VI and his family in the last year of Smuts' United Party government was hailed (wrongly as it turned out) as a great achievement in terms of English–Afrikaans reconciliation. Black African opinion was considered unimportant and insignificant. True, the outside world had received with acclaim Alan Paton's *Cry, the Beloved Country*. The beauty of its prose-poetry; the marvellously compassionate portrayal of its characters, both black and white; the authenticity of its story-line were enough to make it not only a best-seller but a challenge to the minds and consciences of all who read it.

To those of us who lived with its actual situation in places like Sophiatown and Orlando it was something more. For although it was a novel in the Olive Schreiner tradition, it was a plea and a warning against that kind of complacency which would lead South Africa, and possibly the world, to disaster. 'I have one great fear in my heart,' said the young black priest to his white colleague, 'that when *they* are turned to loving, we shall be turned to *hating*.' How to get *that* message across was a real problem! And how to begin getting it across in the Christian church itself was the first task.

For, as always when confronted with a major issue affecting its total membership, the church itself was divided. The Province of South Africa under the leadership of Archbishop Geoffrey Clayton of Cape Town certainly had great influence on both sides of the colour line. Clayton himself, when Bishop of Johannesburg, had taken a strong and vigorous anti-apartheid initiative in his dealings with the city council over 'native' administration. Always in his addresses to synod he had spoken from a strongly theological base against racism in all its forms. He was a very great preacher and a formidable ecclesiastical statesman respected (and often feared) for his forthrightness in both church and state. He did not suffer fools gladly, and even those who were not foolish but were sometimes timid or over-respectful felt the lash of his tongue. And he was by now convinced that, evil as apartheid undoubtedly was, it must be fought (so far at least as the Christian world was concerned) from *within* South Africa. He believed that for Christians in Britain (or, for that matter, in America or New Zealand) to protest about South African affairs would be counter-productive. In his view it would make the task of the local church harder by antagonizing the government. As each new and more vicious law found its way on to the statute book it could and should be opposed by South African churchmen, but not by Christians who had no stake in the country.

So he persuaded the Archbishop of Canterbury – Geoffrey Fisher – that it would be a mistake for the Church of England to initiate or support any programme of open protest, such as the boycotting of sport or cultural activities. Clearly there was a case for this line of argument and it certainly found ready support in both countries and in both parts of the Anglican communion, English and South African. Increasingly, however, and especially after the passing of the Bantu Education Act, there were those like Ambrose Reeves and myself who believed that the only possible attitude open to the Christian church on South African racism was the catholic, universalist attitude which sees racism, whatever form it takes, as inherently evil. And, as a consequence of this, we believed it to be our duty to mobilize world opinion against it.

As early as 1950 Christian Action arranged a public meeting in London for Michael Scott, and in the same year a lecture tour for Alan Paton, including a sermon in St. Paul's Cathedral. This was the beginning of that personal relationship between John Collins and those who were heavily engaged in the battle against racism in South Africa.

It needs to be remembered (and it is not easy to remember) that twenty-five years ago there were very few in Britain who understood at all what was at stake. After all, one of the great war-time leaders, the man who had played a major role in drafting the constitution of the United Nations and whose name had been a household word in England since the Boer war, was a South African. If Jan Christian Smuts was typical of his countrymen, there could not be much wrong with the Afrikaaner. And even if he had been defeated by Malan in the 1948 elections, this was another proof of the essentially democratic structure of the nation he represented. In these years, before even the first successful British colony to seek independence (Ghana) had achieved its aim, there was no public opinion in England expressive of concern for the African peoples.

Yet by 1952, in South Africa itself, the Defiance Campaign against unjust and discriminatory legislation had been mounted on Gandhian lines. It was strictly a campaign of passive resistance in which at first scores and then thousands of non-white citizens (the Asian and coloured communities as well as the African took part) deliberately courted arrest and imprisonment by entering premises, parks, railway stations reserved for whites, or in other ways broke the segregation laws. The campaign was exceedingly effective. The prisons began to overflow. Included amongst those arrested and detained were Patrick Duncan – son of a former Governor General – and Manilal Gandhi, son of the Mahatma himself.

Christian Action responded to the appeal launched by the

Campaign for funds to help the families of those who were in prison. Thus began a pattern of support which has never altered, except to grow in volume over the years in order to meet the ever increasing needs of the victims of state violence.

In November of that same year John preached a sermon in St. Paul's Cathedral which was to have strong repercussions. He described Dr. Malan, South Africa's Prime Minister, as '. . . this poor wretched man hag-ridden with fear'. The correspondence columns of the press at last began to reflect public opinion on the whole vast issue of racism in a Commonwealth country. For the first time since the end of the war against Hitler, British papers were being alerted to the truth that anti-Semitism and the atrocities perpetrated by the Nazis were not the *only* forms of racism alive and kicking in our world. It was realized, dimly at first but with increasing clarity, that Britain – its links with South Africa at every level so strong – had a concern which it could not shrug off. And the sermons which followed from the same pulpit gradually stirred debate and argument in the country at large.

It was in fact the public controversy aroused by these sermons which led a Durban business man in 1954 to invite John Collins to visit South Africa '. . . to see for himself just what was going on'. I remember very well the announcement of this invitation in the South African press and my immediate reaction. It was one of fear and doubt. I was afraid that John might only too easily succumb to the deceptive warmth of hospitality which I knew would be offered him in Natal; that he would see only the surface things in a society well provided with a veneer of western Christian 'civilization'. I was doubtful whether any English ecclesiastic, however well-disposed, could at all assess the reality of such a complex situation in one short visit – more especially when it would make life so much easier to be able to return to St. Paul's Cathedral with some bromide assertions about the need for patience, understanding and the desirability of avoiding rash judgements on situations so much more fraught with the dangers of misrepresentation than elsewhere.

I need not have worried! But then, in those days, I did not know John. Since 1952 Christian Action had pledged itself not only to collect funds for those 'suffering for conscience sake in South Africa' but also 'to bring Christian insights and Christian action to bear upon our responsibility in British territories in Africa'. After his 1954 visit, now greatly strengthened in speaking about

South African affairs by having seen things for himself, John dedicated himself and Christian Action to the campaign which would eventually make it impossible for anyone in Britain to be in ignorance of the meaning of 'apartheid'.

A group of us in South Africa at that time, which included Alan Paton, Rev. Arthur Blaxall, Ambrose Reeves and myself, was able to channel the funds in the right direction – and there was no shortage of urgently needy claimants for assistance. But, much more significantly, those of us who were so actively engaged in the conflict now knew that we had an ever increasing body of support to which we could turn, and that this support group was also our public relations organization. So at last it was recognized that the issues of race and colour conflict in South Africa had to be tackled *not* as issues peculiar to that country, nor as the responsibility of the *local* church, but as a challenge to the Christian conscience of the world.

It is hard to exaggerate the importance of this change at that time. It was in fact a kind of watershed dividing the South Africa of the Empire and Commonwealth (which, to so many Britons, meant simply an extension of their own institutions and structures to the Great Continent) from the South Africa in which the majority, being black, had begun their struggle for freedom and deserved support because they were oppressed. One could say that it was an awakening in every way comparable to that at the beginning of Wilberforce's campaign against the slave trade. And there were in fact close parallels between the two. So many upright and honourable men in church and state opposed Wilberforce and his colleagues, and found moral arguments for doing so, because they had long since persuaded themselves that slavery was part of a divine or providential purpose that had continued through the ages. Similarly in Britain honest men and women in positions of authority and in every sector of society believed it to be wrong to attack the South African Government because it represented authority, law and order, and was so closely involved in the Commonwealth that it must surely be left to manage its own affairs. Although it could not be argued that South Africans were all our 'kith and kin' (as a decade later it was said of the white Rhodesians), there was a strong feeling that the values of the union of Boer and Briton were, in all essentials, the same: and they were *ipso facto* Christian values.

In recognizing, then publicizing and finally actively proclaiming this changed view, John Collins was exercising a prophetic role. And, like most prophets, he had to pay the penalty.

Three events in South Africa marked those years between 1954 and 1956, and in all of them I was closely enough involved to know what Christian Action, under John's leadership, achieved. The first was the passing of the Bantu Education Act. The second was the Western Areas Removal Scheme, and the third was the Congress of the People with its freedom charter, leading up to the Treason Trial.

Dr. Verwoerd stated that Bantu education would stand 'with both feet in the Reserves'. Archbishop Clayton wrote in *Church News* that the reason for the taking over of African education '. . . seems to be not so much that the church cannot do the job efficiently as that the Government desires to make African education an instrument for forwarding the ideas of a European political party. That is the recognized pattern of a totalitarian State. It is the sort of thing most of us objected to in the Nazi regime of Germany'.

Nevertheless the Archbishop, together with most of the other Church leaders, confronted with the appalling choice between co-operation and the closure of all African 'mission' schools ('the throwing of large numbers of children upon the streets') chose co-operation. 'Even a rotten system of education,' he wrote, 'is better than that which young children pick up in the streets, when, as is usually the case, their fathers and mothers have to go to work and cannot supervise them.'

The one exception, however reluctant, in the Anglican Church to this acceptance of the Bantu Education Act was the Diocese of Johannesburg led by Bishop Ambrose Reeves. 'The Church,' he wrote, 'has no alternative but to refuse to co-operate in any way in furthering an education policy which violates the principles from which all true education ought to spring . . . I dare not take the risk that buildings which have been erected by the money and labours of church people may be used to indoctrinate children with a racial ideology which I am persuaded is clean contrary to the Gospel'.

And on April 1, 1955 the Anglican Church in the Southern Transvaal closed all its schools.

This meant that alternative patterns of education had to be found – and money had to be found to embody those patterns in some recognizable way. It was going to be immensely difficult. But

Christian Action arranged a meeting for Ambrose Reeves in London and launched the Bantu Education Fund and a pilot scheme for correspondence courses for Africans who were linked by letter to members of Christian Action with professional qualifications which enabled them to undertake private coaching. This scheme lasted for several years and was undoubtedly of true value at a time when hope was in such short supply for the young, gifted African, and when the use of his own ability and talents was so deliberately restricted by that obscene law.

I would go so far as to say that it was precisely because Christian Action could point to positive *acts* of this kind that not only was its credibility established, but mutual confidence between black African leaders and the Anglican Church was sustained and strengthened. Against the tide of fear and mistrust which always threatened to destroy that trust, the positive evidence of love and concern from Christians in Britain was of incalculable consequence. Now, twenty-two years later, when once again the 'winds of change' are blowing with hurricane force across the African continent, when South Africa is compelled to seek *détente* with its neighbours, and when 'black consciousness' and 'black power' signify a vigorous recovery of morale and point to revolutionary changes within the republic, however unwillingly conceded by the Government, it is good to reflect that at least one diocese of the Anglican communion stood firm on principle. And it may well be that, in the longer perspectives of history, our stand against the Bantu Education Act will be seen as comparable with the stand of the German Confessional Church against the Nazis. Just as then men like Bonhoeffer looked to the Christians in Britain for the wider, more catholic support they needed, so did Ambrose Reeves in his moment of courageous decision. And John Collins, through Christian Action, never failed to give that support.

At the same time as we were having to fight the battle for educational rights and freedoms – the battle for the future of Africa – a bill was introduced by the Government to remove and resettle the entire population of Sophiatown, some 60,000 people, on the grounds that it would be a massive slum clearance.

The real reason for the resettlement bill, however, was that Sophiatown was the only freehold township in Johannesburg, the only place that Africans in the city could call their own.

I have in fact said all I can say about that period of conflict and turmoil in my book *Naught for your Comfort* which was written whilst it was going on around me. I only restate the bare facts here, because once again it was essential that the widest possible publicity in the world press should be given us if were to have any chance of effective witness. And, in my view, this publicity could not have occurred without the years of steady campaigning that preceded it from the pulpit of St. Paul's and the office of Christian Action in John Collins' home in Amen Court. I wonder in fact whether at any time in its history that quiet and lovely Wren house had dreamed of being such a revolutionary place!

It could be said that the worldwide publicity given to the 'Western Areas Removal Scheme', as it came to be known, had no great effect: the people were moved, Sophiatown bulldozed out of existence, and the place, now a white working-class suburb, renamed 'Triomf' (Triumph). Yet, like the Bantu Education Act, it was in fact one of those moments of challenge and choice confronting the church. It had to do not with the physical removal of people from one place to another, but with the meaning of human rights and human dignity. It was symbolic in the highest degree because it demonstrated so clearly the truth about apartheid. These people were the work-force of Johannesburg, the main source of its wealth. Yet they were also the poorest and the most powerless. Sophiatown, with all its overcrowding and squalor, was yet a *community* with a vigour, a warmth, a richness of its own – totally in contrast with the monotonous, soulless, drab municipal township to the west of the city. Their removal was a perfect illustration of the underlying philosophy of South African racism. It was white South Africa saying to black South Africa: 'We want your labour, you kaffirs, we *need* your labour to keep the wheels of industry turning, to get the gold out of the ground, to sustain our standard of living as the representatives of western civilization. Yes, we want your labour, black men, but we don't want *you*'.

They were terrible but exciting and marvellously challenging years. But for me time was running out. The last great event in which I took part before I was recalled to England in 1956 was the Congress of the People described by Mary Benson in these words:

'Let us speak of Freedom!' On Saturday, June 25, 1955, on a battered patch of veld in Kliptown village near Johannesburg, three thousand delegates responded to this 'call', just over two thousand Africans with two or three hundred each of Indians, coloured people and whites. Along the roadside, stalls sold bright soft drinks and mixed confections. One visitor from England thought it more like a black Derby Day than a solemn conclave of revolutionaries, as the crowd rolled up singing, laughing, shouting, wearing gay clothes, men in vivid Basuto blankets and straw hats, women in brilliant saris or in Congress blouses, with a variety of scarves. It was like South Africa in miniature – doctors and peasants, labourers and shopkeepers, ministers and domestic servants, students and city workers, teachers and housewives; and all the races in due proportion. The A.N.C. colours dominated the scene. Banners announced the identity of branches or carried slogans: *Freedom in our Lifetime*; *Long Live the Struggle* . . . The Special Branch, large men in lounge suits, stood at the entrance to the wired-in enclosure of the gathering, taking photographs of all *white* arrivals. As the meeting proceeded they recorded every word – no matter what – and stared fixedly at the platform through binoculars . . .

Throughout that day and Sunday morning the delegates listened intently to a Freedom Charter read in English, Lesotho and Xosa . . . 'We the People of South Africa declare for all our country and the world to know: that South Africa belongs to all who live in it, black and white, and that no government can justly claim authority unless it is based on the will of all the people.'

The Congress of the People, with its Freedom Charter (I have a framed copy of it still) was in fact the precursor of what would happen – with violence and bloodshed – at Sharpeville five years later. The names of those 'whites' who attended that meeting would reappear before that bloody event in the list of persons arrested in 1956 on charges of high treason.

And again, Christian Action immediately responded by launching the Treason Trial Defence Fund. It was certainly needed! The trial lasted four years and, in the event, all one hundred and fifty-six were acquitted. It had cost two hundred thousand pounds and of this all but thirty thousand pounds was produced by Christian Action.

Indeed, it was seen by John Collins as such a vitally significant part of Christian Action's work that in 1958 its terms of reference were extended to cover assistance to those persecuted in Rhodesia as well. 'The Defence and Aid Fund' came into existence to finance the heavy legal costs of the vast number of trials and to support the countless families and individuals affected.

After Sharpeville the Fund was called upon to finance an independent inquiry into the shooting, to support the relatives and children of the victims and – increasingly – to care for the stream of refugees leaving South Africa.

But before all this I had left South Africa myself to face exile. It was in fact leap-year day, February 29, 1956 when I said good-bye to that 'beloved country'. And writing now, twenty years after the event, I can vividly recall the scene at Jan Smuts airport: and I still do not care to write of it.

More easily can I write of the meetings in London when I came to know and love John personally. The great gathering in the Central Hall; the smaller gatherings in Amen Court, when Victor Gollancz, J. B. Priestley and so many others met to invigorate or sustain the campaign.

I am certain that it has never yet been realized as it should by the Great British Public that the conscience of a country on such a major issue as race and colour conflict cannot be stirred to action without the commitment and costly dedication of a handful of individuals.

And I am also certain, and am proud to go on record saying it, that *informed* opposition to apartheid in Britain owes as much to John Collins and Christian Action as *informed* opposition to the slave trade owed to Wilberforce. And when history comes to be written, the name of John Collins will have an equally honoured place.

South African racist policy; the anti-apartheid movement; the consequences for world peace of all that happens in the area of race relations anywhere on earth – all these things twenty-five years ago were of little or no significance to the ordinary Briton. The fact that today they are recognized and acknowledged as urgent international priorities is in large measure due to the unflagging dedication and enthusiasm of one man. I thank God for him.

2 THE BIRTH OF A FUND

Per Wästberg

In the autumn of 1959 I returned to Stockholm after spending eight months of study in Rhodesia and South Africa. Because of my newspaper articles and other writings, my visit ended with my being declared a prohibited immigrant in both those countries, as well as in the Portuguese colonies of Mozambique and Angola.

At the same time Senator Leslie Rubin who represented African interests in the Cape Town Parliament arrived in Stockholm. I had met this active champion of African rights while I was in the Cape, and I immediately sought his assistance in setting up a Swedish Fund for the victims of apartheid. Dean Gunnar Helander, who had spent many years as a missionary in South Africa, took and still takes a very active part in this work.

We gathered together as sponsors a great number of outstanding citizens – cabinet ministers, bishops, writers and university professors – and we launched our appeal. It was the first of its kind in Scandinavia, and money poured in, often from unexpected quarters. Schools performed day-works for the Fund, church collections became a regular source of income (here the credit must go to Dean Helander) and many individuals donated as much as one or even two per cent of their yearly salaries. At first I was not aware of the existence of the British Defence and Aid Fund, so the Swedish money was sent to refugees in Lesotho, to multi-racial schools and to South African deserters and students in Scandinavia.

In 1960 I came to London and it was then that I first had contact with Defence and Aid and with Canon Collins. It was just after the Sharpeville shootings, and I found myself spending a considerable amount of time in the cellars of 2 Amen Court discussing the private consumers' boycott of South African goods, which Patrick van Rensburg was organizing on behalf of the Defence and Aid Fund. A similar boycott had a temporary success in Sweden and served to emphasize the moral importance of resisting trade with South Africa.

Of course while at Amen Court I found my way upstairs into the large study where I had talks with John Collins, and over the years these have continued unabated and unceasingly. I learnt then something of the history of Defence and Aid, and of John Collins' active involvement in Southern Africa since 1950. I learned of the support given by Christian Action (the parent body of Defence and Aid) to the families of the African passive resisters in 1952, and in particular I learned the history of the notorious South African Treason Trial which had lasted four years and had cost £100,000 – nearly all of it raised by the personal effort and energy of John Collins. This trial had just been brought to a triumphant conclusion with the acquittal of all one hundred and fifty-six of the accused. During those four years what had begun as the Christian Action Treason Trial Fund had become the British Defence and Aid Fund, ready to come to the assistance of all genuine victims of apartheid without any distinction of race, creed or political affiliation.

As I first made contact with Defence and Aid it was being almost overwhelmed by the tragic consequences of the Sharpeville shootings. Money was pouring in, a considerable amount coming from overseas, and as much as £40,000 was raised in a single month. The Fund was supporting the families of all killed or wounded at Sharpeville, and it was financing an independent legal enquiry into the shootings. At the same time it was supporting the large numbers of refugees who had fled from South Africa to what were then the Protectorates of Basutoland, Swaziland and Bechuanaland, as well as to Ghana and Tanganyika.

From that time onwards the Swedish Fund began channelling its money through the British Defence and Aid Fund with which I remained closely associated.

In 1961 John Collins, together with the late Robert Resha of the African National Congress, visited Sweden and appeared on television, as John Collins has done many times since. By 1966 protests against the American involvement in Vietnam had begun to take over the political scene, but up to then the anti-apartheid movement in Sweden was the largest expression of public opinion on any international issue. This popular pressure, and an increasing commitment to newly decolonized Africa, led to the formation by the Swedish Government of SIDA, an agency for assistance to developing countries. Within this agency, a commission was appointed to study relations with the expatriate African liberation movements of South Africa and Rhodesia. This commission, of which both Gunnar Helander and I are members, now presses for and (with the approval of Parliament) channels humanitarian assistance to these same liberation movements. SIDA is supported by all parliamentary parties from the conservatives to the communists.

Meanwhile the Defence and Aid Fund became more and more firmly established on the international field. In 1963 came the Rivonia Trial, once more financed by Defence and Aid. This trial, which received worldwide coverage, ended with the passing of life sentences upon Bram Fischer, Nelson Mandela and Walter Sisulu. Soon after this, the General Assembly of the United Nations passed a resolution urging member governments to contribute money for the relief of victims of apartheid. This resolution, among other events, led to the foundation of the International Defence and Aid Fund (IDAF).

Headquarters were established in London where the British Fund undertakes all administration. Initially there were six affiliated committees: Sweden, Norway, Denmark, Australia, New Zealand and the United States. These have now been joined by Eire and Holland. The UN sub-committee on apartheid nominated IDAF as one of three bodies suitable to receive donations from UN member states, and the Fund is now among those non-governmental organizations enjoying consultative status with the Economic and Social Council (ECOSOC) of the UN, and with UNESCO.

The first governmental grants to IDAF came in 1965: £35,000 from Sweden, £10,000 from Holland, £10,000 from the USSR and £2,000 from India. These countries were followed by the Philippines, Denmark, Kenya, Iran, Morocco, Sudan, Pakistan and Norway.

In 1966 the UN set up its own Trust Fund for Southern Africa. In the same year, South Africa banned all Defence and Aid Committees working in that country. Although IDAF had no organizational links with South African Committees, it has had to abandon public appeals and depends increasingly upon the support of governments and the UN Trust Fund. In the years 1967–1975 approximately one million pounds was donated by governments and the UN Trust Fund, and half a million pounds came from private sources.

The British reader may well be wondering why the Swedish people and the Swedish government feel such a strong commitment to the abolition of apartheid and the liberation of Southern Africa. It is easy enough to understand the reactions of individuals who like myself have seen at first hand some of the cruelties and injustices of apartheid, and the degree to which that racist system crushes and deforms human beings of all colours. It is easy too to understand the ready response from church circles, especially since for many years the Swedish churches have supported a large-scale missionary activity throughout Southern Africa. But what of the government?

Sweden, of course, has a democratically elected government, and this must be sensitive to public pressure and public concern, but its attitudes also go back into the roots of Swedish history. Since battling for its independence against Danes, Germans and Russians, Sweden has enjoyed one hundred and fifty years of peaceful neutrality. Non-alignment, independence of power blocs, instinctive support for the self-determination of peoples, a kind of natural anti-colonialism – all these are so much a part of Swedish consciousness that they are not even matters for discussion; they are simply part of what is.

During the eighteenth and nineteenth centuries Sweden could easily have become a colonial power; territories on the Gold Coast and in the West Indies were hers for the asking, but the memories of her own struggle for independence were too strong, and she refused. In our own days these attitudes have been reinforced by the appearance on our borders of a new colonialism that has already engulfed the Baltic republics of Latvia, Estonia and Lithuania. The invasions of both Hungary and Czechoslovakia also strongly affected public opinion.

A small country, opposed to power blocs, naturally finds its best outlet for international activity through the UN. Perhaps more than any other figure in modern times, Dag Hammarskjöld expressed most clearly in an international context concern for the rights and freedoms of small nations.

No Swedish government can, or would wish to depart from the traditional policies of political and military non-alignment. But this does not mean that Sweden has to possess a moral neutrality. Quite the contrary; since the last war, a strong feeling has grown up, especially among students and young people, that the very advantages that Sweden enjoys, its relative affluence, its advanced welfare state, constitute in themselves an opportunity and an obligation to take a moral stand upon important international issues. Far from there being any resentment at the amount of money allocated for overseas aid, the government is under considerable pressure to allocate even more.

Governments, like individuals, run into all kinds of contradictions and ambiguities when they attempt to take a moral stand in politics. Take, for instance, the question of armed force. Sweden sincerely desires and is prepared to work for the liberation of Southern Africa; but she is also concerned for peace. Her humanitarian assistance to the African liberation movements must and does stop short of the provision of arms or of money to buy arms. Regrettably Sweden, like other nations, plays some small part in the general, international, commercial traffic in arms. Her compromise is to try to sell only to countries that are at peace.

Then there is the vexed question of investment in South Africa. Sweden of course supports the UN sanctions against Rhodesia. However, there have been a small number of Swedish firms operating in South Africa for several decades. There is a good deal of public interest and agitation centred around these firms, especially in regard to the wages and welfare benefits paid to their non-European workers. The government does not forbid investment in South Africa but it is officially opposed to any new investment. No government money would be forthcoming for any such venture, which means that Swedish industrialists are unlikely to make any easy profit in that part of the world. A compromise? Perhaps. A trades union delegation recently visited South Africa to investigate working conditions in Swedish firms operating there. It has reported that, unless conditions are very much improved within three years, the Swedish government should be asked to withhold permission for Swedish firms to operate in South Africa. Another compromise? We shall see.

With this background it is easy to see why the Swedish government has found IDAF such a valuable instrument to which to give its support. Here is an independent humanitarian and international organization led by a churchman of integrity and of international repute; an organization that has been involved in various aspects of South Africa for more than twenty-five years, and an organization which is supported and recommended for support by the UN. And while the Fund has never been identified with any one area of the political spectrum and gives aid without discrimination, it also has close and friendly links with leaders of the various liberation movements, who have time and again expressed their appreciation of the unique work of the Fund and the need for its extension.

At the meeting of the UN special committee on apartheid in Dublin in 1974, the chairman H. E. Ambassador Edwin Ogebe Ogbu asked every member of the UN to contribute to IDAF and said:

> The Special Committee would like to place on record its recognition of the historic service performed by the Reverend Canon L. John Collins in support of the millions of oppressed people of South Africa for over two decades.
>
> He has stood by the people of South Africa, and their liberation movement, in good times and bad. He has not wavered at any time, even in those crucial periods when other people claiming to be the opponents of racism have hesitated. We know that this noble activity has involved a great strain and great sacrifice. At the same time, we know of the gratitude of the South African people and their liberation movement to Canon Collins. We would like to add that he has performed a service not only for the people of South Africa, but also for the universal cause of freedom and human dignity.
>
> We hope that he will receive increasing support for the International Defence and Aid Fund so that he can meet all the needs in the struggle for freedom in Southern Africa.

Since then, Ambassador Ogbu has written to every member state of the UN asking for direct contributions to IDAF, even though many member states have already donated to the UN Trust Fund.

The aim of IDAF is to contribute to freedom and human dignity in Southern Africa and it distributes money strictly within its terms of reference:

1. To aid, defend and rehabilitate the victims of unjust legislation, oppressive and arbitrary procedures.
2. To support their families and dependents.
3. To keep the conscience of the world alive to the issues at stake.

But for all its humanitarian emphasis, John Collins has never attempted to hide the political nature of the Fund. He never ceases to point out that within the context of apartheid, humanitarian aid is also inevitably political. Actions which in any sane country would be regarded as acts of charity or simply good-neighbourliness can, in South Africa, be branded as acts of 'terrorism' or 'communism'.

As President and Director of IDAF, John Collins has had to wrestle with the contradictions and complexities of such political activity as his conscience drives him to undertake. When Christian Action first gave its support to the ANC led by Chief Lutuli, ANC's policy was a Ghandian one of non-violent resistance to unjust laws. After the Sharpeville massacre, the African liberation movements abandoned their policy of non-violence and decided to counter violence with violence. This shift presented many Christians and pacifists with a sharp dilemma. John Collins, though remaining personally a pacifist, refused to abandon his humanitarian assistance and pointed to the extreme violence executed by the apartheid regime. Who indeed in our so-called civilized world can, in this matter of violence, cast the first stone? Hardly Mr. Vorster who intends to enforce the permanent inferiority of the black man to the white, hardly anyone of east or west, who enjoys the benefits of a civilization largely rooted in violence, nor yet any member of the Christian churches whose records are so red with blood.

It is from his insight into the human suffering of all those who are oppressed in Southern Africa that John Collins gets his restless energy and his outstanding ability to get things done. In his opening speech to the Twelfth Annual Conference of IDAF in Dublin in May 1975 he said:

We meet with a sense of urgency in the knowledge that every year that passes is another year of wasted life for those brave men and women who spend their days in South African gaols for no other reason than their refusal to remain passive under a racialist tyranny; it is another wasted year for all who are banned and detained, and for all children and young people who are denied education and opportunity simply because of the colour of their skins; it is another year of deprivation for all the thousands who are daily denied many of even the most elementary of human rights.

The practical help given by the Fund in terms of legal defence and material aid sustains the morale of all those who oppose and those who are victims of the white minority regimes. This humanitarian assistance rendered by IDAF does not pretend to solve the problems of Southern Africa, nor to assist (except in a minor way) in the development of a non-racial democratic society. These problems can be solved only by the black majority and all other groups now oppressed. Whether this will be done in a non-violent way or not is not for us outsiders to decide, but we may influence events by continued support to all those who in their resistance to the evils of apartheid seek to create a new South Africa where the majority will be able to decide its own destiny in peace. We recognize – as John Collins has also remarked – that peace cannot be bought at any price.

A peace that is not securely based upon freedom and justice, upon human rights for all, is no peace at all: it is merely a buying of time in the hope that the inevitable suffering and violence that result from oppression and injustice will fall on shoulders other than your own.

One aspect of the work of IDAF, repeatedly emphasized by John Collins, is that any vestige of paternalism, any attachment of strings, any consideration of self-interest in the provision of aid will not do. Only by giving the liberation movements the humanitarian aid they need, by sharing with them in their struggles, can the international community demonstrate the sincerity of its professed belief in a non-racial democratic Southern Africa.

From 1965 the Swedish government's yearly decision to support IDAF has been unanimous. The confidence of the government in the work of the Fund and in Canon Collins personally is evident in the increasing grants which now total about £150,000 a year. Sweden also gives some support to Amnesty and the World Council of Churches for their work in Southern Africa, and contributes as well to the UN Trust Fund. But it has always made clear that it sees IDAF as the principal receiver of donations and the most reliable distributor of legal and humanitarian aid.

The ways of distributing aid to those who need it most must, for obvious reasons, be kept secret. It is a measure of the trust that many governments put in the person of Canon Collins and in his staff that they do not ask for knowledge of how their money is being channelled.

I have acted as a kind of unofficial assistant to John Collins and as a go-between or explanatory messenger between IDAF, the Swedish affiliated fund and the Swedish government. Thus I have experienced Amen Court in all states of calm and uproar, with revolutionaries, cabinet ministers and bishops coming and going, arguing with one another, and I have heard all sorts of African leaders discussing these problems in the large study of John Collins, with the chimes of St. Paul's Cathedral clock punctuating our conversations and reminding us of our earthly shortcomings.

1 NO ROOM AT THE INN

Ian Henderson

Quite fortuitously when I began writing this essay, I found that my copy of John Collins's autobiography *Faith Under Fire* was sitting next to Attwater's *Dictionary of Saints* on the bookshelf! Because the former reinforces my own impression of John as a great human being, established through thirteen years of friendship and working partnership, I began to reflect on how many of the saints in the official Kalendar of the church would measure up to the same judgement. And I decided that several would, but many wouldn't. Is sanctity, in any case, about humanity? In fact, I have stumbled unwittingly into one of the great debates of Christian experience which is no less contemporary today than the moment when St. Augustine of Hippo splendidly affirmed that grace perfects nature. St. Augustine, despite the bad press he gets over unbaptized babies, was a great Christian humanist. Many Christians were not and are not humanists. The doleful Cornelius Jansen, who claimed to be Augustine's disciple, taught the fundamental antagonism between grace and nature and the virus he communicated is still in the bloodstream of both Protestant and Roman Catholic Christianity. Its persistence explains not only the absence of a rich humanity in the character of several official saints but it also underlies the scepticism in many quarters of Christendom about the compatibility of humanitarian social reform with the purposes of God. It is an attitude expressed across the wide spectrum of theological sophistication from Malcolm Muggeridge's barbed shafts at *Guardian* leader writers to the fulminations of the Doomsday men on Epsom Downs.

John Collins and Christian Action commended themselves to me by their espousal of humanitarian values and, what is more, by their willingness to see humanists as allies in the struggle. Humanist values, they seemed to be saying, are also Christian values. Advances of civilization were welcomed because they were civilized. Uncivilized and retrograde movements were condemned because they were uncivilized and productive of human suffering and not simply because they inconvenienced the church. I remember hearing a prominent Christian layman addressing the congregation of my own church in the course of which he mentioned apartheid. It seemed unfortunate but significant that his real objection to that doctrine was that it separated black from white worshippers in church. John Collins on the other hand has stood out against apartheid from the beginning because it was an affront to human dignity and this affront was just as shameful on a park bench as it was in a church pew.

There are many causes that John Collins embraced which illustrate his concern for human values and his alliance with other humanitarians of both religious and non-religious inspiration. The Campaign for the Abolition of Capital Punishment was one important example. So too was the Campaign for Nuclear Disarmament (CND) which is fully described and analysed elsewhere in this book. I would like to select another example of this endeavour which has offered less scope for John Collins's crusading style but has nevertheless become one of the most enduring achievements of the movement which he founded. This is the work of Christian Action generally performed under the title of Homeless in Britain.

Homelessness is no new social phenomenon. In fact, the continued existence of thousands of homeless and rootless people in our community despite the massive social changes of the last seventy years is a cause of surprise and shame. Admittedly, as I have tried to show elsewhere, the social aetiology of the problem today is different from that which characterized the homelessness to be found in the Victorian cities. Admittedly John Collins and Christian Action are not the only people in our generation to be moved to action by the wretched spectacle of the homeless. Nevertheless Christian Action brought to bear some new insights into the problem. It was also among the first to harness the enthusiasm of young people into this highly practical expression of the gospel of love even if many, perhaps most of them, would not formally recognize the connexion between the Christian gospel and their own personal commitment.

Homelessness, like poverty, was said by some political wisecracksmen to have been rediscovered in the 1960's. The emergence of this fairly old-established problem in a new guise has been blamed on a variety of causes: the activities of a new breed of landlords like the late Peter Rachman, for example, or immigration from the Commonwealth, or migration within the United Kingdom. All these factors are not, of course, causes but symptoms of the main cause which was the economic boom of the late 1950's and which put intolerable pressure on the inadequate and aging housing stock of London and most of our major cities. One of the first studies in depth to be published at that period – the Milner-Holland Report (1964) – came to this conclusion and could furthermore see no immediate alleviation of the problem. This was at a time when J. K. Galbraith, writing about the American urban scene, spoke memorably of a situation of 'private affluence and public squalor'. Market forces by themselves may produce increased automobile ownership and a multiplication of the range of dog foods but they do not produce good low-rent housing, new hospitals and an adequate public transport system. Because the public sector was starved – and despite, monetarist politicians may say, still is starved – of resources, the local authorities (in London's case, the old LCC) were ill-equipped to cope with the emergency. Hence the indignities of places like Newington Lodge and other inadequate attempts to care for homeless families.

The association between homelessness and the details of the Christmas story is too close to avoid exploitation, and just before Christmas 1962 the Bishops of London and Southwark led a march to St. Paul's Cathedral which they called 'No Room at the Inn'. The marchers offered no specific political or short-term solutions to the problem of homelessness which was reckoned to be running at the rate of five thousand homeless individuals in the LCC area alone, but they did attempt to focus concern on the problem. It is worth noting how the Aldermaston-style march, pioneered by CND and John Collins, was becoming the accepted mode for social protest at that time and had even found favour with the establishment. It was in fact the official representative of the Archbishop of Canterbury on the Council of Christian Action (at that time a prominent layman in the Diocese of Southwark) Uvedale Lambert, who first suggested to Christian Action that it ought to become a vehicle for increasing public concern about homelessness. One inhibiting factor was that housing as a subject had for long been part of the auction room of election promises.

Figures for housing targets had been bandied about by both the major political parties ever since the war, both sides trying to suggest that the official figure represented an overestimate or an underestimate, according to your party political standpoint. So the mere involvement of Christian Action in that kind of slanging match wasn't going to help a great deal. This is why the idea of a housing 'pressure group' pure and simple was rejected and a new fund initiated which would support practical work in the field as a supplement to the campaign to arouse public opinion.

Homeless in Britain – at that time the Homeless in Britain Fund – was launched in the autumn of 1963 and aimed at raising an initial target of one hundred thousand pounds by the fairly lavish use of newspaper advertising which had been so notably successful in gathering together funds for the defence of political prisoners in South Africa. How was the money to be used? Various ideas were put forward from the somewhat short-term suggestion of building new and better hostels to an intensively funded campaign of pressure on statutory institutions already mentioned. In the end Christian Action decided to use the long-established machinery of the Housing Association movement which had the advantage of using charitable funds to generate statutory funds – what is known in housing finance as 'pump-priming' – and also enabled the new fund to help a variety of projects at the same time.

Later on Christian Action moved into the Housing Association business itself, establishing some two dozen housing associations throughout the United Kingdom. My geographical definition is deliberate because one of the first Christian Action Housing Associations to come into existence – in 1965 – was in Glasgow and arose out of close relationship with Christian Action developed with a mixed Presbyterian–Episcopalian group ministerial team known as the Gorbals Group Ministry. This worked at that time in what a national newspaper report had called the most notorious slum in the northern hemisphere. The group ministry had strong similarities with the East Harlem Protestant Parish, a remarkable ecumenical experiment in down-town New York which has been memorably described in a book entitled *Come out the Wilderness* by a Church of Scotland Minister, Bruce Kenrick.

In fact Kenrick had come back from his sojourn in New York and settled in London's Notting Hill, cited by the Milner-Holland Report to have the most overcrowded and dilapidated housing in

London, where race riots had flared up during the hot midsummer of 1958. Here he decided that the quickest way of increasing available housing stock was to renovate old housing and convert it into family flats available at low rents. Kenrick was also one of the first to point out that London's homeless constituted a far greater body than that suggested by official LCC statistics. Thousands of people in Notting Hill were living in conditions which were, in reality, indistinguishable from homelessness. Bruce Kenrick, by then a member of the Council of Christian Action, came to see John Collins and asked if the money could be raised for the first house for the newly-founded Notting Hill Housing Trust. The money was raised with all the alacrity that had characterized the fund-raising for the Defence and Aid Fund for Southern Africa eight years earlier. The first house was bought – in Blenheim Crescent, only a few hundred yards from an even more famous street, then called Rillington Place. Kenrick and his fellow trustees, however, had ambitions to generate similar projects to the Notting Hill Housing Trust in other badly housed parts of London and several provincial cities. Some of the money acquired was used to make more money by launching a national fund-raising campaign initially for Notting Hill but with the declared objective of extending this activity over a national sphere.

It is interesting to speculate whether the early Homeless in Britain Fund could have been more effective if it had remained linked to the Notting Hill Housing Trust and its plan for housing development in all the housing black spots in the United Kingdom. Here was an area in which John Collins, hard pressed on so many fronts, especially by the growing volume of work which the Defence and Aid Fund was creating, had to rely on the advice of others – and sometimes this advice was conflicting. Furthermore the Homeless in Britain Fund had decided to establish its sphere of interest as widely as possible and this entailed concern for the single homeless whose problems were fundamentally different from homeless families (although they were persistently confused by the media and, worse, by many statutory bodies). It was, I suppose, due to my own influence, as the member of Christian Action's staff charged with overall responsibility for the Homeless in Britain Fund, that the movement gradually focused all its attention on the single homeless. Christian Action Housing Associations, by the very fact of their constitution, slowly became autonomous, and in 1966 Bruce Kenrick and others from the Notting Hill Housing Trust called together a consortium of movements in the housing field – they included Christian Action, the Catholic Housing Aid Society and the British Churches Housing Trust – and proposed the establishing of a new national campaigning organization which would also raise funds for the Housing Association movement in the four black spot cities of London, Glasgow, Liverpool and Birmingham. This campaign, which was christened *Shelter*, soon became the wonder-baby of post-war charities. For this it deserves credit, but it should be recorded that its financial success was partly due to the gentlemen's agreement whereby the participating organizations, including Christian Action, waived their right to make public appeals on a national basis for their own Housing Associations.

Christian Action's new interest in single homeless persons brought it close to an area of activity which had interested John Collins as early as the 1940's. This was penal reform and the attitude of society to the offender. John Collins had, from long personal experience as a priest, come up against the pathetic social and personal inadequacy which is so often the background to petty crime. The reform of penal institutions and methods was essential for a more compassionate, understanding attitude to this sort of social casualty, but society's treatment of the unemployable inadequate, the psychopath, the alcoholic and the rootless personality also required scrutiny.

One man who happened to be embarking on a great personal journey of faith at about the same time as the Homeless in Britain Fund was set up was an ex-Bow Street probation officer, Anton Wallich-Clifford. He had begun to penetrate the dark jungle of seedy streets and bombsites where the jack drinkers and winos hung out – vagrant alcoholics addicted to cheap wines or cider more often than not fortified with methylated or surgical spirit. Wallich-Clifford, a devout Roman Catholic who had been strongly influenced by the Houses of Hospitality in the Bowery and other down-town American urban areas started by the American Catholic Worker movement, began some experiments with this kind of sheltered accommodation in Britain. Like Bruce Kenrick he turned to Christian Action for financial support which brought several people in Christian Action, not least myself, into close contact with Wallich-Clifford, his philosophy and his unorthodox but brilliant methods.

Despite its early financial and its continued moral support for

Wallich-Clifford's Simon Community, Christian Action decided to venture into the field of provision for the single homeless person, having become especially interested in the problems of homeless women whose numbers were always underestimated in the official surveys of those who sleep rough and for whom provision was scanty. After commissioning a survey of women sleeping rough on or near Waterloo Station, Christian Action opened a Shelter for Women in Lambeth High Street which was a mere gin bottle's throw from Lambeth Palace. Like all such experiments it made mistakes in its early days, but it would not be true to say of the shelter, as David Brandon says in his book *Homeless*, that it was a conventional hostel with a set of rigid rules, aimed at excluding certain categories of women. Although the first senior social worker attempted to apply a measure of selection in relation to her intake due to the unexpected demand, itself an indication of the gravity of the problem, within a very short time admission policy was non-selective and the shelter became known for its willingness to accept women who had been blacklisted at almost every hostel in London.

The shelter at Lambeth was discovered by the playwright Jeremy Sandford, author of the television play *Kathy Come Home* which dealt with hostels like Newington Lodge. After several months of research at the Christian Action shelter in Lambeth, Sandford produced his prize-winning play, *Edna, the Inebriate Woman* which succeeded as perhaps few other modern creative works have done in communicating something of the bizarre world of homeless isolates, and one attempt to reach out to them.

Christian Action was, however, concerned with more than providing shelter for a few homeless women. During the late 1960's it endeavoured to investigate its cause. Like Anton Wallich-Clifford and the Simon Community it maintained that vagrancy today springs from social causes different from those of vagrancy in a previous era and that, far from being an obstinate hangover from the old society that the welfare state and Keynesian economics helped to destroy, vagrancy is in fact a creation of contemporary society. And this society, let it be added, is one from which the majority of the working class have derived large-scale material benefits.

The price we have paid for these material gains has been the destruction of community, the whole complex network of local and family relationships that gives significance to human existence. Marx used the term 'alienation' to mean the lack of identity that a person had with his work in a capitalist society. A lesser-known contemporary of Marx, Ferdinand Tönnies got nearer the truth when he described the process whereby the *Gemeinschaft* (community) is overwhelmed by the demands of the *Gesellschaft* (society). While he pointed out that all social relationships must be compounded of both elements, he prophesied the increase of social anonymity that industrialism and urbanization would bring. His analysis is a vindication of the modern 'small is beautiful' movement.

The fact that there is a connexion between the ecological crisis and the problems of urban deprivation, including vagrancy, is recognized in the now famous issue of the *Ecologist* magazine which was later reprinted as *Blueprint for Survival*. It provided a clue for those pioneers in the care of social drop-outs, who saw the need for more than social security payments and the provision of reception centres. The need was to enable rootless men and women to rediscover community while at the same time working for political social changes which would enable the systematic destruction of organic community to be halted and reversed. In this respect there is an interesting link between Christian Action's Homeless in Britain work and its sponsorship of the London School of Non-Violence which is associated with the review *Resurgence* and the writings of E. F. Schumacher.

The Christian Action shelter in Lambeth developed in time into a complex of projects designed to meet the needs of homeless women. The main functions of the Lambeth shelter were transferred in 1971 to a former girl's residential club in Soho where a new kind of therapeutic community was established and is described in some detail by David Brandon in *Homeless* and other articles and pamphlets. A small second-stage house was opened in the East End of London to help women with a specific alcoholic problem. Homeless in Britain was also one of the pioneers of work with single homeless men in Birmingham. An advice centre and soup kitchen was set up in the centre of the city as far back as 1969 and later a residential hostel was opened in Edgbaston. The local Christian Action committee which was set up to administer the projects has now become wholly independent of Homeless in Britain.

One of the many modern developments of Homeless in Britain

was its help with the foundation of the first co-ordinating body for work with homeless single persons, CHAR (Campaign for the Homeless and Rootless) which continued on a wider front the campaign of public education about single homelessness. The late Richard Crossman was perhaps the first Secretary of State for the Social Services to engage in an ongoing dialogue with Christian Action on the treatment of single homeless men and women, and it was as a result of such conversations that an enquiry into the psychiatric facilities available in government reception centres was initiated. Today the Department of Health and Social Security not only helps to fund many projects administered by Homeless in Britain but is involved in regular discussions with it and other voluntary bodies about the quality and volume of care available through both statutory and voluntary channels.

One of those who battled most doggedly for the derelicts of Victorian London was William Booth, founder of the Salvation Army. Yet he is recorded as saying that the only real good you can do to a man is to save his soul. I remember some years ago addressing a group of local Anglican clergy about the work that Christian Action was doing in that area for homeless single persons and being roundly challenged by a clergyman who believed that evangelism – 'providing a personal introduction to our Lord and Saviour' – should take precedence over the satisfaction of material wants. He was answered by another member of the audience who suggested that there was sound Biblical evidence for believing that the practical care and concern that Christian Action was exercising was just as much a form of evangelism as the distribution of tracts.

This incident and the whole attempt to assess the achievements of Homeless in Britain leads me to ask the question: what if anything does distinguish the care and compassion of the Christian from the humanist? The only answer that I have come up with has no connexion with any dualistic notions of souls and bodies. It is in the duration of Christian love and hence in its quality. No experience can teach you about human fallibility as that of working with social deviants. In ordinary case-work terms the backsliding of the psychopath, the chronic alcoholic, the recidivist can easily tempt even the most painstaking physician or social worker to believe that such people are hopeless cases. The Christian, it seems, must persist perhaps even irrationally, because he believes that he serves Christ in even the most abandoned of 'these my brethren' and because he is committed to a belief in the infinite power of love.

Christian Action has perhaps more consistently than any other community of Christians in my own generation displayed unwavering commitment to the gospel of love, not (as John Collins himself wrote) an 'unattainable ideal, but the only realistic way of life for mankind'.

2 THE VOICE OF AN ERA

Mervyn Jones

The story has often been told: at the founding meeting of the Campaign for Nuclear Disarmament (CND), held in January 1958 at Canon Collins' house in Amen Court, Kingsley Martin said briskly, 'Let's have Bertie Russell as president and John Collins as chairman'. In the light of later events, it may not have been one of Kingsley's best ideas. The notion of an active chairman and a more honorific president, on the lines of a royal personage designated as patron of something like the Red Cross, reveals the conventional groove in which the minds of the CND founders were moving at that time. But I still think today that the choice of John Collins as chairman had a certain inspired inevitability. I also think that he was being handed an ultimately impossible job, truly a bed of nails.

I make both these statements because of the complex and many-sided character of CND, which of course was only dimly apparent when it had yet to hold its first public meeting or appeal for support. In the course of the next couple of years, we who were active in it grasped that complexity with a sort of bewildered awe. CND was a moral crusade, it was a mass movement, it was the instrument of a political programme; it was a social phenomenon, it was an intellectual trend, and it was also a litmus test of beliefs and personalities, in that by knowing the mind and spirit of an individual one could know whether he or she would be in CND or not. There has been nothing quite like it in our times, and it is impossible to convey to younger people the nature of the experience that we – joyously, passionately, but also laboriously – went through. However it was also the kind of thing that happens recurrently in England; and one of the reasons why I honour it and miss it is that it earned England the admiration of large numbers of

Europeans and Americans, a fact to be wistfully recalled in the late 'seventies.

The movements that have left this kind of memory have always appealed both to conscience and to common sense, thus attracting those who are strong on the former and also those who are strong on the latter, as well as types who combine these characteristics such as Oliver Cromwell. Such movements have been authentically democratic while also being an arena for unusual, indeed eccentric and uncompromising personalities; hence they have been unruly and difficult to guide. They have been rich in paradox – hence the campaign against the slave trade, with which CND was often compared, was a radical movement led by a man who in many ways was a profound conservative. In all these respects CND was in the true English tradition. And John Collins is, among other things, a very English sort of man.

CND was a coalition, and could not have amounted to anything without being a coalition. But merely to list the elements in this coalition is a task of elaborate and subtle analysis. To preside over them was a formidable assignment indeed.

There were people who were simply outraged by the inhumanity and wickedness of nuclear bombs. For them, to protest against such weapons was a straightforward assertion of their own decency. It had nothing to do with politics, as they conceived of politics, and for the most part these people had never been involved in political action and didn't wish to be. But of course the fact that CND could arouse the feelings of such people and draw them into taking a public stand on a public issue was what made CND significant, and forced the politicians to pay attention to it.

There were people who, with equally genuine emotions about the wickedness of 'the bomb', saw the renunciation of nuclear weapons as part of a world policy which they already favoured: disengagement in Europe, the winding up of the strategic bases of the great powers, non-alignment for Britain. Active and experienced members of the Labour Party and of trade unions, these people were the Bevanites of the previous decade, and greatly regretted that Aneurin Bevan had not chosen to come out against the bomb when it was a key issue at the 1957 Labour Party conference. (If he had, CND would have been quite a different movement.)

There were people such as Sir Stephen King-Hall, a member of the original CND committee, who considered that for Britain with its obvious vulnerability to maintain an independent deterrent was an irrational defence policy. For them it was a question of logic, and indeed of expert knowledge. Generally, they saw nothing wrong with the deterrent in American hands or with NATO, and had no wish to see Britain adopt a new stance in world affairs.

There were people who, whether actually communists or not, counted themselves as pro-Soviet and were against the bomb (British or American) as an instrument of the cold war – a threat to the Soviet Union which they regarded as a peace-loving nation. Since the Soviet Union was a nuclear power and responsible for some of the more horrendous nuclear tests, this attitude was under suspicion in CND circles, though no more so than the attitude of the King-Hall wing. Some of these people, however, were in the Labour Party and opposition to the cold war was common to them and to the Bevanites; anyway, a communist has as much right to be appalled by the prospect of nuclear war as anyone else, and if the CP moved towards supporting CND (very reluctantly at first) this was probably from fear of losing its troops.

There were pacifists who had long been opposed to all kinds of armed force and who saw CND as an extension of their basic outlook. Some of them indeed held aloof from CND and endorsed, from a contrary standpoint, the argument of defenders of nuclear weapons that you couldn't be against the bomb unless you were equally against the rifle. But most of them came into CND, where they constituted a kind of elect, disdaining to use the standard CND argument that the bomb was a qualitatively new form of genocidal violence.

There were people who, while opposed to orthodox forms of political activity and scornful of elections and governments, nevertheless had their own channels of political action as anarchists or members of small radical groups. For them the bomb was a monstrous excrescence of the state, and CND was an opportunity to challenge the state at a vulnerable point. They joined with others – sometimes with no political allegiance and few political ideas – for whom the challenge was authentic only if it led to breaking the law on every possible occasion.

There were Christians, including many ministers of religion, who were impelled to raise their voices against the bomb through their conception of the faith that they held and also their conception of the duty of the churches (including their personal duty) as the moral counsellor of the nation. Some of these Christians were pacifists, some were Labour Party activists, and some were linked to figures such as Canon Collins through having spoken up on other issues, such as apartheid.

There were non-Christians who came forward in opposition to the bomb as an application of the sceptical and rationalist tradition. For them the bomb was an absurdity as well as an evil, and CND was a mobilization of the reasoning mind.

There were writers and artists whose imaginations were stirred by the emotional and moral upsurge. In the more serious cases, the CND message expressed their profoundest idea of the value of human life and the principles that should inspire it; and they were intuitively aware that they couldn't stand aside (and they could indeed learn) from a social phenomenon of this kind. However, an element of superficial trendiness was also to be observed. As friends gathered round their picnic baskets, it was inevitable that someone should describe the Aldermaston march as 'the Ascot of the left'.

There were students and other young people for whom opposition to the bomb was a repudiation of official dogma and unquestioning obedience to authority. ('The establishment' as a term in everyday use dates from the same period.) CND from this angle was a means of liberation from the dullness and conformity of the 1950's. England was a different place in those days, and I can remember earnest expressions of disapproval – from veteran socialists, quite often – of the young men with long hair and the 'indecently dressed' girls, the steel bands that followed the march, the dancing in lunch breaks, the kiss that might catch the eye of a press photographer, all seen as inconsistent with the serious purpose of saving mankind from annihilation. If CND had not contained this element it might have guarded itself from some attacks and gained greater support in some quarters; but then, if it had not contained this element it would not have been the movement that it was.

Amid this variegated scene, and symbolically at the head of the march each Easter, there strode the figure of the canon with his cassock, his spectacles and his amiable smile. To some he was unconventional – canons are not usually found leading marches – but to others he was archetypically conventional. To some he was accommodating himself to a fashion, but to others he was confining a popular movement within what repetition made into a ritual.

It was said that he was offering a dangerous and anarchic diversion from serious politics; it was also said that he was providing a lightning-conductor to avert a truly radical assault on authority. Clearly, he couldn't win.

Still, he was the right chairman because he represented many of the elements in CND – he was a Christian, he was a pacifist, he was a Labour Party supporter, he was to a certain degree pro-Soviet and certainly an opponent of the cold war – and he was able to show a ready comprehension for those elements with which he was not identified. He genuinely liked young people and never condescended to them; he enjoyed the company of writers and artists and understood how their minds worked. He also understood the motives and the temperament that impelled a wing of the campaign towards civil disobedience. He was capable of tolerance, and of charity in the true sense, but also of a rarer quality: an intuitive sympathy with anyone acting from sincere principles, even when he thought the resultant action ill-advised. This quality often stood him in good stead, but it sometimes landed him in false situations; after he had emphatically expressed his respect for the civil disobedience enthusiasts, they were disillusioned to find that he didn't really agree with them. But he could not, being the man he was, have behaved in any other way.

As well as the diverse and at times chaotic character of CND, one other factor made leading the campaign an impossible job. This was its impatient, indeed apocalyptic outlook. The great majority of the Aldermaston marchers believed that nuclear war was likely to break out at any moment, in other words that their lives or the lives of their children were in imminent peril. A series of books and films gave vivid expression to the impending horrors which were stressed at every CND meeting. Anyway, nuclear tests were actually happening and were causing an unknown number of people (but some people, certainly) to die of cancer and leukemia. I don't think that CND was wrong to call attention to the danger of war (which was real, in my opinion) nor to alert public opinion to the devastating power of the bomb, which too many were ready to accept as just another weapon and as a plausible means of national defence. And of course this sense of desperate urgency was just what enabled CND to gain the ear of thousands who are apathetic in the face of ordinary political oratory. Clearly, however, there was an intense pressure on the part of the rank and file for results. Inevitably, the leaders of the campaign, mostly people who were no longer young and who devoted part of their time to other activities, were accused of not trying hard enough. The obvious target for criticism was naturally the chairman.

Besides, most of the leaders – including John Collins – believed that renunciation of the bomb meant renunciation by the British Government, and that the essential precondition was the election of a Labour government. Large sections of the rank and file didn't believe this; or if they were at first prepared to accept it, they were in no mood to wait patiently for another five years when the Tories were returned in 1959. In 1960 renunciation gained the day at the Labour conference, but Hugh Gaitskell refused to bow to the verdict and got it reversed the next year, which appeared to prove that CND had spent its energies on a useless game. Once again, that was the chairman's fault.

I don't know what would have happened if the chairman of CND had been a person of inspiring authority and dominant will. An explosion, I dare say. Anyway, that was not John Collins' personality nor his chosen style. He was modest, rational and persuasive; he listened to what others said and took advice; he laboured to achieve compromises; he retreated from positions that proved to be unpopular. Probably no one else could have held CND together as long as he did.

But it was precisely his good qualities – and, to express my personal view, his likeable qualities – that aroused antagonism. He had skills that gave an impression of the smoothly professional; he was a good chairman of conferences and a good committee man. He liked to arrange matters peaceably and avoid clashes, so he would have a quiet word with delegates of whose attitudes he had been informed and suggest that they should intervene at a given moment. He also liked small talk, jokes, informal social gatherings, wine and cigars. He had personal friends in the movement, and it followed that there were people who didn't possess (and mostly didn't seek) his friendship. He was on good terms with the press. To the suspicious and puritanical elements in the movement (and there were plenty of them) it appeared that he was what they most distrusted – a politician. His flexibility was interpreted as insincerity; his readiness to compromise was taken to imply that he would abandon any principle to keep the show on the road and to preserve his own position.

John was also modest and discreet about the fact that he is a Christian, and this was probably a mistake. The matter is a fairly

78

subtle one, about which I write with some caution since I am not a Christian myself. The balance between evangelism and ministration, or in theological parlance between faith and works, is a theme on which Christians have disputed for centuries, nor does a recourse to the sayings of Jesus seem to give indisputable guidance. In the Church of England – which has always been a state church involved in temporal matters, and which in this century operates in a predominantly non-believing country – the tradition of concern with aspects of life that are not directly religious is well established. Ministers devote their time to housing problems and youth clubs (or sometimes to racial equality and nuclear disarmament) rather than to propagating their beliefs. This is a wholly honourable and of course socially useful way to behave. Paradoxically, however, it does not earn them the respect of non-Christians, who tend to feel that a truly convinced Christian ought to come on like Savonarola. Charity, mildness and attempts to refrain from hatred also don't, alas, make the favourable impression that they should. When I became involved in CND, I soon observed that whereas John Collins found the Rev. Michael Scott (distinctly a Savonarola type) exasperating, Michael Scott simply hated John Collins. I also observed that the militants of the Committee of One Hundred, who were no more Christians than they were Moslems, much preferred Scott.

John was naturally aware that most of the founding fathers of CND – Bertrand Russell, J. B. Priestley, Kingsley Martin, Benn Levy, Michael Foot and the secretary, Peggy Duff – were not Christians. On the whole they were identified with what I have called the sceptical and rationalist tradition in English intellectual life. However, they were his friends, and the value he places on friendship is amongst his most attractive characteristics. As the movement grew, it attracted a considerable amount of Christian support; but it also attracted very many non-Christians – the radicals, the straightforward political types, the writers and artists, and the thousands of young people who had simply grown up in an environment to which religion was an irrelevance. Was he to lecture all these people and tell them that they ought to be Christians? Clearly, no. John Collins is a very nice man.

Although I saw a good deal of John, socially as well as on political occasions during the CND years, I never heard him speak of religion until that period of both our lives was over. I brought it up myself, I'm afraid out of sheer curiosity, and he talked for the

79

greater part of an evening about Christian doctrines (the resurrection figured prominently, but I must have brought that up too) with unmistakable sincerity and fervour. I said to my wife as we went to bed: 'What do you know, John believes in all that stuff after all.' I felt extremely moved and rather ashamed of myself, as one does feel when one has drawn another person into revealing what is deeply important to him and inherently private. In the fundamental sense, like many men who enjoy conviviality and talk, John is a shy man. This is one of the English things about him. (I write as a Welshman.) I wish now that, once at least, he had talked about the resurrection over coffee after a CND executive committee meeting. He could have convinced the members that he believed in it, and that he was not merely a politician.

This leads me to reflect, finally, on the relationship between the political and the moral aspects of the CND movement. My friend Benedict Birnberg, who was secretary of a large CND group, had a list of members and marked their names with either a P or an M. This over-simplified the matter, but it was surprising how few borderline cases there were. In Benedict's definition, a P was someone who considered that nuclear disarmament would be achieved by political action of roughly the same type as that conducted by existing parties and pressure groups. Had John been in that local group he would have earned a P.

The injustice (not on the part of Benedict Birnberg, who was just enjoying himself, but on the part of a number of people in CND) was to suppose that a P could not also be an M. What I believe – and, though I cannot quote him, I think that John believes the same – is that moral principles should govern political decisions, and not only the great decisions of history but also the housing policy of the borough council; that the proper aim of public activity is not to keep morality immune from politics, but to infuse morality into politics; that parties, candidates and governments are to be judged precisely on the moral content of their actions – judged, but also influenced and helped.

In the end, I don't think that any other attitude is valid. It is possible to withdraw into a private pursuit of sanctity and disclaim all responsibility for the state of the world; it is possible on the other hand to get so involved in the political process that one accepts its standards and renounces one's own. At all times, John Collins was aware of both dangers, or it might be more accurate to say both temptations. The path that he chose to follow, in CND as well as in Christian Action and in the whole of his public life, is necessarily difficult. One has to make complex decisions, to accept disappointments, to reckon with the certainty of being misunderstood and misrepresented. CND was a challenge, willingly and courageously met by many, but by none more so than John Collins. It was, at the best moments, an exaltation; and it was also an ordeal. I admired him then, and I honour him now, for the resolute and faithful way in which he went through it.

PART THREE

CHRISTIAN ACTION AND CONSCIENCE

1 MATTERS OF MORALS

The Earl of Longford

The life and role of Canon John Collins are of special interest under at least six headings. I am trying to write of him dispassionately, prescinding (as theologians used to say) from my long standing admiring friendship with him and Diana Collins, his partner in everything. I am drawing heavily on his own vivid and eloquent autobiography *Faith under Fire*. It was written ten years ago; the achievements of Christian Action have gone forward steadily since then. Penal reform and the care of the homeless are two instances of many which could be mentioned.

The book cannot, naturally, refer in terms to John Collins's outstanding gifts of creative leadership. But there the record speaks for itself from the times of the groups or fellowships initiated in wartime. On Christmas Eve 1942, the commanding officer informed John Collins that he wished seats reserved in the front row for him and some of the senior officers at the midnight choral Eucharist.

> I reminded him that since the Fellowship had come into being, we did not recognize rank at specifically church functions, that I hoped he and his colleagues would remain sober and that, in any case, they ought to arrive in good time as seats could not be reserved.

The C.O. came, and the story had the happiest of endings. Who else would have pulled that off except John Collins?

Subject to the qualifications indicated, the book seems to me to give a remarkably accurate picture. It certainly does not conceal what an awkward customer John has proved himself on occasion to various notables, from Archbishop Fisher downwards.

The headings I would select are these: first, the theological position at which he has arrived after much intellectual and spiritual travail and long reflection on his varied experience. Second,

85

his attitude to the church, to which he has dedicated his professional life and of which he is still officially a prominent representative. Third, his creation and inspiration of Christian Action for
close on thirty years, starting from nothing and carrying on to the
point where its permanency seems to be assured. Fourth, his leading part in the promotion of certain far-reaching causes. The most
prominent have been, in the first instance, the fair treatment of
Germany, later racial justice and world peace, with special stress
on nuclear disarmament. Fifth, there is his special relationship
with leading humanists and other non-Christians in the propaga-
tion of those very causes; and finally, his general view of the
relationship between religion and politics.

Perhaps the first two headings, his Christian beliefs and his
attitude to his own church, can be taken together. He begins his
book by telling us that his friends sometimes ask him, 'Why don't
you get out of the church?' 'You don't believe in half the things the
church stands for, but you daren't say so.' He is admittedly hostile
to authority, in all its recognized forms. He refuses absolutely to
believe anything because it is laid down for him by others. One
cannot help wondering whether he would secure ordination today
if he presented himself as a candidate for the first time. But no one
who knows him or reads his book can doubt his persistence or
the sincerity of his devotion to the church to which he has
many reasons for gratitude and to which he has, in his own
fashion, rendered such signal service. He himself sums up in this
way:

> If I am wrong in the ways in which I try to fulfil my ministry as a
> priest, it is for the church to repudiate me; I could not repudiate the
> church.

There is mercifully no prospect as far as I am aware of the church
doing anything so foolish as to extrude John Collins.

It is abundantly clear that he has never wavered, and does not
waver now in his loyalty to the deepest truths of Christianity.
'Despite,' he affirms,

> the apparent evidences to the contrary, I believe that God is love.
> For the Christian the over-riding loyalty must be to Christ . . .
> Because I believe that Christ gave us the clearest manifestation of the
> true nature of God yet seen in history, this highest loyalty of the
> Christian, to which all others must be subservient, is in reality a
> loyalty to God. But because I also believe that man is made in God's

86

image, an over-riding loyalty to Christ also means for me an over-riding loyalty to man in God's image, to man as seen in Christ, to man irrespective of his race, creed, colour, nationality, occupation or family.

All that is straightforward and orthodox Christianity. Bishops and archbishops, and John Collins is not very keen on either, could hardly dissent from it, as far as it goes, though they might not think that it went far enough in regard to Christ's divinity. It is worth noting that Christ figures essentially in the chain of reasoning. Certainly John Collins himself, highly inspirational, has always drawn a supreme inspiration from Jesus. John Collins therefore sallies forth to struggle with the problems of the world from an inner fortress of basic Christian belief. He has rebelled increasingly against the clerical establishment, moving from an inside to an outside position as time has gone on. But he has never rebelled against the most fundamental Christian doctrines.

Christian Action was born out of the historic meeting in the Oxford Town Hall on October 5, 1946. The meeting, like so much else to follow, was initiated and masterminded by John Collins. It was heralded as a call for Christian action in public affairs. There was no limit to the width and depth of the aspiration opened up. But John Collins had as a result of his experience in the R.A.F. come to believe that the most effective way of spreading a general idea was to demonstrate its truth as applied to particular situations. 'By their fruits you shall know them.'

The special action which flowed from the Town Hall meeting was a desperate effort to bring justice and humanity into our treatment of stricken and starving Germany. The response was immediate and the impact lasting.

I will not linger over the many other initiatives of Christian Action described elsewhere in this book. I pass on to John Collins's association with stirring causes, sometimes representing Christian Action, sometimes operating individually. I have only space to cover two – racial justice and world peace, though one must at least mention his great work for the abolition of hanging.

Here the present writer's approach becomes inevitably subjective. Some of John Collins's causes seem to me 'good' beyond question, in the sense that no Christian should ever have questioned them, or question them today. Older people are beginning to forget, and younger ones were never aware of the treatment intended for Germany under the Potsdam Agreement. She was to be held down indefinitely and though the terrible hunger of the years up to 1948 was not intended by the western allies, it was an inevitable consequence of the refusal to introduce a real currency for three years after the war, for fear of offending the Russians.

John Collins is entitled to say that the churches collectively were far too sluggish in denouncing the horror of what Victor Gollancz exposed more effectively than anyone. But the conscience of the churches, asserted initially by the Bishop of Chichester, was always in advance of that of governments. Countless Christians, clerical and lay of all denominations, laboured without stint to rescue the Germans. John Collins does not seem particularly keen on Moral Rearmament, but their services were quite outstanding in the darkest period.

The point I am making here is that in the case of Germany the Christian task was intellectually simple, because once Christians were alerted they could not fail to be on the right side. But to take two other causes, racial justice and world peace, the thing has been much more complex, though of course all right-minded people must desire both with all their hearts. The heroic and prolonged audacity of John Collins in his dealings with South Africa and Africans generally has already won him an immortal niche in the African memory.

But in the moral sphere there have remained difficulties not only on the tactical but on the strategic plane, if one may use such terms in regard to morals. When African leaders, as described in his book, decided at a certain point that violence was necessary to secure freedom and justice, it was not (and is not) by any means obvious that all good Christians had to agree with the support John Collins gave them. It may be said that nothing he said or did was intended to encourage violence, even in pursuit of a legitimate objective. He was concerned only with the legal defence of those accused and arrested. I am not trying to judge that question here, merely to draw the distinction between this issue and that of Germany where, putting it crudely, the moral arguments were all on one side.

Still more glaringly do we encounter an inevitable clash between enlightened Christians when we come to CND, whose story is told here absorbingly. In this case it was not only the official clergy who stood aloof, it was the majority of Labour M.P.s and a high proportion (which cannot be calculated) of Christian socialists like myself. We did not then, and do not now believe that – leaving out

John Collins for the moment – those who led the CND marches were any better qualified to provide moral (or for that matter any other kind of) guidance to the nation. The antics of Lord Russell are dealt with charitably here, but he and others like him proved an all too significant element in the crusade. When we pass from personalities and move on to the deepest level of moral argument, we soon find ourselves back at the endless argument between pacifist and non-pacifist Christians. Of course I am aware that the coming of nuclear weapons brought in a new dimension and, I would agree, strengthened pacifist arguments. But deep down the same issue is at stake, as anyone will recall who heard Bevin and Lansbury at the Labour Conference in 1935. I can still feel the thrill pass through us all when Lansbury quoted the words 'those who take the sword will perish by the sword'. He was overwhelmed when it came to the vote, but the issue is never disposed of.

John Collins deals with the pacifist dilemma with noble frankness. I call it noble because at a certain point he casts aside discretion and asks himself the question 'Do I contradict myself?' He supplies the answer: 'Very well, then, I contradict myself.' Personally I do not think that he does. As I understand it he is really saying that in the last resort men and women must come together and agree in a spirit of Christian love at any given moment on the course to follow. At the same time he rules out certain methods (nuclear warfare, for example) as intolerable under any conditions. There is nothing illogical about this approach. But that does not make it logically coercive, or force all Christians of goodwill and intelligence to accept it meekly.

It is no criticism of Christian Action to say that they have not had the resources to deal with more than a few questions in a large way. If Stafford Cripps, the grandfather (as John Collins has been the father of Christian Action) had lived, it may be that they would have handled what politicians at the moment would call 'the central issues' – income distribution, industrial relations and the rest. A good many Christians including myself will regret their inability to come out fairly and squarely against pornography and, for that matter, to say anything helpful about abortion. But I must restrain myself here. Nothing infuriates me more if I am tackling, shall we say pornography, than to be asked why I am neglecting prisons; and if I say that I have been concerned with them for the last thirty years, to be told to find something more significant than either. Let us be profoundly thankful for what Christian Action has accomplished in these last thirty years and let us hope that in the next thirty they will be able to cast their net still wider.

More than once in his book John Collins mentions the strong friendships he has formed with leading humanists as a result of the CND operations. His attitude to co-operation with humanists will hardly seem novel to Christians who are well accustomed to working with pseudo-Christians, non-Christians and anti-Christians on the political level. However, I find him ambivalent towards the comparative morality of Christians and non-Christians. At times in his book he indicates that Christian belief is an essential element in the conviction that ultimately the reign of love will prevail. Yet at other times he seems to me to lean over too far backwards to admit that non-Christians are just as full as Christians are of the Christian virtues. He and others in this kind of argument always seem to me to be comparing the best humanists with the average Christians and to be carrying to rather absurd lengths the Christian virtue of humility.

Coming to the question of religion in relation to politics, what considerations arising from the thought of John Collins have we not touched on? Out of many arresting sentiments, I pick out one almost at random:

> It is because I believe that the community life of man is a shadow of the life of that city of love to which the Christian Gospel points, that I am convinced that we have to take our religion into politics and, indeed, into every sphere of life where relationship is significant.

That is well and truly said and I agree with its spirit totally.

In his recent book of memoirs, some parts of it of real spiritual value, Lord Hailsham argues in a contrary sense. He agrees, of course, that a Christian should behave as such in politics as in any other profession. But he does not agree that Christian notions can be directly applied to the formation of the good society. Here I side emphatically with John Collins. Societies don't form themselves and operate themselves by accident. It is our communal responsibility to decide for example whether the richest one per cent of the community should possess ninety per cent of the wealth, or fifty per cent, or for that matter one per cent. As Christians we cannot escape our share of that responsibility in proportion to our numbers of possible influence.

A special question arises whether the clergy, collectively or individually, should step forward boldly into the arena of political controversy. On the one hand there is the disadvantage of a bishop or lesser clergyman dividing his flock by adopting a loyalty to one party rather than another; on the other hand there is the impossibility of a man filled with the spirit of the Lord keeping silent when evil is afoot. John Collins is the first to recognize that many different vocations are available to the dedicated priest, some of them in a political sense much more controversial than others. For myself, I could wish that we had still more men like John Collins, Trevor Huddleston and Donald Soper, to mention only three, and that the churches were readier to take larger risks in public debate without actually committing themselves to a party allegiance.

Since the book under discussion was written, the author has established further claims on the esteem of all who are thrilled by the sight of a Christian conscience expressing itself without regard to personal consequence. John Collins has kept the faith and will go on keeping it. He has fought the fight and will go on fighting it. Even his friends will seldom think that he is altogether right, and a few others will assume that he is usually wrong. Long may he continue on his way, basing his actions on his beliefs and his beliefs on what he considers to be the teaching of his Master.

2 MATTERS OF POLITICS

Richard Acland

In the early months of 1947 John Collins was the anonymous author of an interesting pamphlet; and the anonymity was preserved until he revealed his authorship in 1966 (in *Faith Under Fire* (Leslie Frewin 1966), pages 131-2). I shall start from this pamphlet first as a tribute to John, next as a peg on which to hang some reflections on the relation between religion and social problems which has been his deep concern throughout his working life; and last but not least, as a prelude to an essay in self-glorification.

I met John for the first time when he asked me to speak to the R.A.F. and W.A.A.F. at Yatesbury where he was chaplain. I remember no word that was spoken either way; I recall only a sea of Air Force blue; it was at a time when the Forces were very interested in Common Wealth. John and I found that our religious and political ideas were congenial, as they have been ever since; and we kept in touch through the period that led to the formation of Christian Action in Oxford on December 5, 1946.

A few months later, the King designated Sunday July 6, 1947 as a national day of prayer and dedication. Pressed, I think, by Stafford Cripps, the Archbishop of Canterbury felt that there ought to be a pamphlet of some kind to guide the nation's spiritual endeavour; and he invited John to write it anonymously. In his foreword Geoffrey Fisher says, and this I vividly remember, that the whole was written 'in a great hurry and under great pressure' and that the anonymous author 'had sought the advice of a large number of his friends'. I do not know what other friends advised him; I submitted a draft of the section headed 'Economic Crisis'; though I cannot now tell which sentences are mine, which mine amended by John and which wholly his.

The Archbishop had insisted not only that the author himself be anonymous, but that quotations, if used, should have no foot-notes by which their authors could be identified. This is sad, because I should now like to know which 'American observer' said:

Britain is the only nation in the western world which has a fair chance of composing the great debate (whose) issue . . . is this: how can one achieve justice without sacrificing freedom in a modern technical society?

I also wish I knew who wrote another pregnant passage:

The gravest danger to social health and harmony comes from the belief of the workers that opposition to their legitimate demands is clothed in sanctimonious phrases about freedom . . . You will never convince the bulk of the population of the importance of liberty . . . until you convince them, by espousing their claim for equity, that you are not using 'liberty' as a catchphrase for reaction . . . For its own sake, the church *must* dispel the impression that it is 'in on' this deception; for society's sake the church must admit that this deception is being used, and denounce it.'

Go to it, Archbishops! Denounce Mrs. Margaret Thatcher and Sir Keith Joseph or whoever has replaced them when these words are read. The whole of John's 1947 pamphlet reads today with astonishing modernity because it was written in the same kind of epoch. It was written just before the years when we had 'never had it so good'; and now we have left them behind. It is worthwhile to understand why that was, and is our situation. 'Our present crisis' (this is either John's writing or his adaptation of mine) 'hits the ordinary man where he feels it. He can't get the things he wants.' John offered three reasons for this: first, the inter-war years which 'the locusts had eaten'; next, wartime physical destruction and the sale of overseas investments; and lastly 'the present trend of world trade'. This raises today a fascinating question to which we have given too little attention. Why, from 1951 to 1972, was it that we had never had it so good? Without British capitalists seriously investing (as their German opposite numbers did) in the modern-ization of the nation's capital equipment, without anyone working harder, without any remission of any restrictive practices, why could we enjoy an almost annual increase in Gross National Product or in the total British 'Cake' as it can be less technically described? For one reason only. Through those years world prices for manufactured goods were relatively rising, while those for raw materials and foods and fuels were relatively falling. The opposite process was at work from 1945 to 1951; and is at work today; and will almost inevitably persist into the future. If anyone can explain the mystery of 1951–72 on any other terms than that foods, raw materials and fuels were then put on to the market by many ill organized little sellers and bought by few well organized western buyers, I shall be glad to hear about it. In the situation of 1945–51, which has recurred today and will dominate the future, some of John's words deserve re-hearing. Here are a few of them (within which I shall not indicate most omissions or trivial words added to carry the sense over sentences that are dropped).

> To see the inconveniences and austerities of the present time in this wider setting is to make it possible to accept them joyfully. In the last century the free play of economic forces arranged that, in the event of shortages, the poorest should get none and the richest most. In recent years we have decided that we should like to see the common cake more fairly shared . . . those who have previously enjoyed the largest slices will have to be content with less. History has created a situation whereby the common cake for this nation may become smaller rather than larger. The plight of Britain is small compared with that of many other countries. She must share fully in the far greater sufferings of others, else irresistible forces will pass stern judgement on her. We must remember that for many years our common living standards have been sustained in part by millions of coloured people working for us at wages and in conditions which we should have repudiated as impossible for ourselves. Speaking as Christians we can be absolutely certain that such a situation ought not to endure. It is essential that we consider all the problems of poverty, shortage and social inequality, not from a national, but from a world viewpoint.

In a six-hundred-and-fifty-word gallop through a thousand years of history, John saw feudalism in which theoretically each found status in an ordered society at the cost of what we now call freedom; and he saw individualism giving freedom at the cost of our no longer living in a meaningful society. Encouraged by his unnamed 'American observer' he wrestles with the resultant problem and quotes two other unnamed authorities: 'Our civilization,' wrote one, 'is in danger of perishing for lack of . . . a deliberate and avowed sense of moral purpose, involving the call for common sacrifices for the sake of the common good.' 'By a beautiful alchemy,' wrote the other, 'which may suggest to us very dimly the hidden meaning of Unity and the Whole, the practice of selfless co-operation ministers, as nothing else can minister, to the serene development of our own personality.' The first of these two comes from E. H. Carr (in *The Conditions of Peace*, Macmillan 1942, page 111) and the second from Victor Gollancz who foreshadows the shorter and widely known slogan 'union differentiates' from Pierre Teilhard de Chardin (see *Christianity and Evolution*, Collins 1971, page 117 footnote). But at the end of the struggle, John finds human morality too weak to take the strain. And had it been his purpose to commend Christianity to non-Christians he would here have fallen into grave error. 'It is for the overcoming of that weakness,' he says, 'that we need to turn again to God for strength.' But one must never ask anyone to believe in Christianity *because* it will help to solve social problems if he does.

John can be excused because the Archbishop had asked for something addressed not to non-Christians but to those who called themselves Christians already. To those he addressed a stirring appeal for personal involvement in social endeavour. Christians believe the world belongs to God; wealth is therefore to be fairly shared. All are sons of God; claims to privilege must be abandoned. Christians know the fact of sin and the need of forgiveness; so we can fight confidently against the results of sin in the world. Men's souls are not saved by schools or hospitals; yet in Britain in the past and in other lands in 1947 Christians built schools and hospitals in the hope that the heathen, seeing their building, would also see Christ at work in the world. For the same reason Christians in 1947 should be seen to be engaged in the social effort to reconcile freedom and justice in a technological society inevitably prevented from enjoying unlimited material abundance.

In days when already large numbers of ordinary irreligious people were dropping out from any kind of involvement in major social problems because the forces on the other side seemed too strong and the chances of 'victory' too remote, John ended his section on Christian revelation with sentences as relevant to the 1970's as to the 1940's:

Because of his faith, the Christian is not concerned, when making his decision for action, with what may or may not be the actual material outcome in the future. He hopes for a result which would commend itself to a secularist; and, as far as possible, he plans and directs his work in order to assist to that end. But he does not depend upon the actual result of his action for his motive for doing it. He does his work for the sake of what it is, and because it is implied in his faith . . .

The fact that he and his work and all who have been affected by it may be physically wiped off the earth tomorrow can make no difference to his resolve to do it. His faith in the great dogmas of Christianity is his only ground for his thought and action.

The pamphlet ended with a section on practical steps as relevant now as it was then. But what happened next? I became involved in other cares and cannot now remember noticing any consequence of the pamphlet to which I had made a modest contribution. John tells me it got good reviews in the religious press and was noticed favourably if briefly in national newspapers of the day. But it takes more than that to shift the Church of England. The authorities sanctioned a first print of 5,000 and when these were sold enquirers learned that the pamphlet was not available. I feel guilty of disobedience to one of John's suggested practical steps: *Be there!* Had I been more on the spot I might have forced a reprint by pressure through the Parliamentary Socialist Christian Group which I had been able to join at about that time. But now I should like to reflect on thirty years of Christian Action experience to which this particular pamphlet made but a trivial contribution. I am not attributing any blame to anyone in relation to any of the major Christian Action decisions. Indeed, how could I? At the time I shared in making many, and I did not dissent from any. With hindsight I simply want to speculate: if we had to do it all over again with the knowledge that is ours today, should we do it in the same way, or differently?

Christian Action set out to be open to Christians of all political parties; and a number of Conservatives and Liberals joined and worked hard. It is true that far larger numbers stayed out, and Christian Action has almost always been an offence to the church establishment. That is greatly to its credit. Without going so far as to say that everything that offends the scribes and Pharisees is right, we can be sure that anything is wrong that does not from time to time offend most of them.

But I wonder. John and I were socialists at the time; and so were many, though doubtless not quite all of those who took a prominent part in launching Christian Action. Would it have been better to have instigated, in 1946, a Christian Association capable of undertaking all the work that Christian Action has in fact undertaken, but also quite openly intended as a rallying point for Christians who were ready to proclaim themselves democratic socialists? With hindsight my answer today is 'Yes'.

96

This pushes me back to the antecedent experience with Common Wealth. As far as I was concerned, Common Wealth was never pre-planned. It grew out of a developing situation. In its heyday it was a small, exciting political party advocating the common ownership of all significant productive resources on moral, not economic grounds. Many, though not all of its members found that Christianity gave them their political motivation, and that a determination to achieve common ownership in the twentieth century could be based on Christian principles. What we proved was that a small political party could advocate common ownership with a dab of religious motivation, and could flourish and could change people's opinions, and perhaps in a small way even influence the course of events, *so long as the major parties were not fighting each other at by-elections*. Our experience further proved that when the large parties resumed their normal activities, the small one was sunk without trace. Putting it in very crude arithmetic, Common Wealth had been at best 75 per cent controversially political and 25 per cent moral (or one might say spiritual, religious or Christian).

What would have happened if there had been founded in 1946 an association with the emphasis the other way round – 75 per cent on religion in general and Christianity in particular, and 25 per cent on controversial politics? It would have been an association aiming to persuade by both the words and the actions of its members; but it would not have been aiming at political power for itself either immediately or at any future time. Its ranks would have been open to people concerned for the religious dimensions of living and firmly convinced that a point had been reached in history at which it had become necessary that in due time the whole of privately owned money-making Big Business must be brought to an end.

The standard objection to this sort of proposal is that it would have involved Christians in political controversy and this, it is held, would be unchristian. Surely this view is only tenable by those who know little Christian history. What about the Christians who lived from AD 600–1100? They lived through a long struggle between roving piracy and some kind of social stability. During the early centuries they could not help knowing that the pirates, though probably fewer, were more powerful than the majority longing for stability of some kind. No one then thought that Christians should be neutral about the major political issue of the day. R. H. Tawney writes of the church of those days that it 'had been engaged in an immense missionary effort, in which, as it struggled with the surrounding barbarism, the work of conversion and of social construction had been almost indistinguishable' (*Religion and the Rise of Capitalism*, Penguin 1938, page 34).

This does not say that feudalism was in any sense eternally justified on Christian principles. It only means that the Holy Spirit, alive and active in the historic situation of that day, was *at that moment* challenging people to end barbaric piracy and initiate *some kind* of social stability.

So what of today? I am not in any way suggesting that common ownership is eternally justified on Christian principles, but I constantly quote those powerful words from *Diagnosis of our Times* (Kegan Paul 1943) by Karl Mannheim: 'Only if the rebirth of religion, both in terms of popular movement and of regenerated leadership, coincides with the forthcoming social transformation can it happen that the new democratic order in this country will be Christian.' Then what is the nature of the 'forthcoming social transformation' in the situation of today? What – not in the ninth or tenth but in the twentieth century – is the Holy Spirit now challenging us to do? If Mannheim is right we must try to answer such questions as these; and it is very unlikely that the answers will win equal approval across the whole spectrum of party political opinion. This means that the rebirth of religion cannot take place unless some Christians will stand up and be counted on issues of major party political controversy.

It would have been enormously important for the suggested association to avoid the disastrous error perpetrated by propagandists in the Labour Party and in the Communist Party and by me in my Common Wealth days. We are all now paying the grievous penalty for having said, or (what is exactly the same thing) having implied, that socialism or even the nationalization of a few industries would *automatically* create a wonderful new sense of social responsibility. That it has wholly failed to do so has persuaded many otherwise intelligent people that ownership, whether private or public, is an irrelevance. This is of course a state of opinion very desirable by those who actually own. The fact still remains that a determination, in due time, to achieve the whole of common ownership, though in no sense the *causa causans*, is certainly now the *sine qua non* of any future sense of social responsibility.

As well as John's leaflet, I think another document from a slightly earlier year can bear re-reading today. It is the addendum to William Temple's 'Malvern Findings' for which Kenneth Ingram and I were responsible. The important parts of it were as follows:

> There is no structural organization of society which can bring about the coming of the Kingdom of God on earth . . . since all systems can be perverted by the selfishness of man. Therefore, the church as such can never commit itself to any proposed change in the structure of society as being a self-sufficient means of salvation. But the church can point to those features of our existing society which, while they can never prevent individual men and women from becoming Christian, are contrary to divine justice, and act as stumbling-blocks, making it harder for men to live Christian lives. In our present situation we believe that the maintenance of that part of the structure of our society, by which the ultimate ownership of the principal industrial resources of the community can be vested in the hands of private owners, *may be* such a stumbling-block . . . While these resources can be so owned, men will strive for their ownership for themselves. As a consequence, a way of life founded on the supremacy of the economic motive will remain, which is contrary to God's plan for mankind. [My italics.]

For the sake of unanimity we weakly accepted 'may be' instead of 'is', after a far more crippling amendment had been carried against us by a majority of about 3:2. But that two-fifths of those who attended the Malvern Conference were fully with us in 1941 suggests that there could have been a significant membership for the sort of association that I am suggesting in the light of the thirty years of experience that have been ours since 1946.

What might the association have achieved? What might its members have done through their active lives? I think they might have affected political power in the only way in which relatively small numbers of people can affect it. This way has been superbly described by J. M. Keynes who wrote the following words at the end of his book *Economic Consequences of the Peace* (Macmillan 1920):

> The events of the coming years will not be shaped by the deliberate acts of statesmen, but by the hidden currents flowing continually beneath the surface of political history, of which no man can predict the outcome. In one way only can we influence these hidden currents – by setting in motion those forces of instruction and imagination which change *opinion*. The assertion of truth, the unveiling of illusion, the dissipation of hate, the enlargement and instruction of men's hearts and minds, must be the means.

I should not have expected any very great results to have shown themselves openly during those slap-happy 'Macmillan years' when the terms of trade moved relentlessly against the world's poor. But now, as in 1945–51, the terms of trade are moving against the world's rich. One cannot expect to convert Conservatives and Liberals 'at a stroke'. But what about the dawn of doubt? Let it be granted that individualist capitalism, as described by the classical economists of the early nineteenth century, was the only social organization through which the Industrial Revolution could have been got off the ground. Let it further be granted that the vast industrial corporations which have dominated our social life through the whole of this century constitute the only possible organizations through which the potentialities of the Industrial Revolution could be most rapidly exploited. Perhaps future generations may wish that these potentialities had been exploited rather less rapidly. The dawn of doubt may arise as we find ourselves irretrievably in the new epoch when increasingly rare and expensive foods, fuels and raw materials impose an absolute veto on increased material consumption in the western world. This, it will be recalled, was the epoch into which John supposed that we had already entered when he wrote his pamphlet at the Archbishop's request. May it not be that privately owned money-making Big Business, so well adapted to conditions that allowed for persistent growth in G.N.P., will be found – is being found – totally incapable of dealing with the situation of today? Of this situation Charles Luce writes: 'If we are to preserve a habitable earth, we must be willing to accept fewer goods and services'. Charles Luce is not of course some romantic environmentalist; he wrote as president of what is probably the largest energy generating corporation in the world. The challenge of our times – the challenge which today is being directed against us by the Holy Spirit – could have been confronted now more hopefully if there had been amongst us, through the last thirty years, an association primarily concerned for religion in general and for Christianity in particular, but incidentally proclaiming that we have reached the point at which Big Business must be ended on moral grounds.

Perhaps, as we did not establish such an association thirty years ago, we might consider establishing it now.

3 MATTERS OF PROTEST

Jacquetta Hawkes

'But what a fanatic the man must be!' I can always recall this exclamation uttered by Norman Collins, his shocking-blue eyes staring with indignation. I stared back – in amazement. Could he really be speaking of John Collins? This was at the height of CND success when the famous resolution in favour of British unilateral disarmament had just been adopted at the Labour Party Conference of 1960. I was then very much involved with the Campaign; at meetings and on the Aldermaston march I had seen John with exemplary patience trying to control extremists of all kinds. I know very well how our true fanatics and firebrands regarded the Chairman. They thought him far too moderate, Christian and law-abiding. Indeed his determination that the law should not be wantonly broken by protesters within a democratic society had just been put to the test by the formation, unknown to him, of the Committee of a Hundred with its policy of civil disobedience.

I must remember this moment so vividly because it sharply exposed what from outside appears to be a contradiction in John: that he has so often led protests against authority, has so often roused the indignation and dislike of the establishment, yet in the very essence of his being is gentle, humorous, reasonable, friendly, and ready to compromise if what is important is not sacrificed. He is always (I truly believe) driven into action by love of the best in man without any trace of the hatred that so inevitably comes to burn in the fanatic or of the enmity in the 'born rebel'.

In fact John was neither born nor grew up as a rebel. To be assured that 'fire-eating John' (as he was once called at Oriel) did not develop this taste as a result of any innate or youthful frustrations, one has only to consider his life story. He was born into a strongly conservative and Conservative family, baptized into the Anglican Church, and his favourite childhood hymn told him that 'The rich man in his castle, The poor man at his gate, God made them high or lowly, And ordered their estate . . .' His call to the priesthood began in admiration for a good and devout parish curate, and at a tender age he was praying that one day he might be Archbishop of Canterbury – in the belief that the higher one rose in the church the holier one would become.

Nor was this only a childish dream. The earlier part of his career was clearly pointing towards high office. Even before he had served his first full year as a deacon he was invited back to be chaplain of his college at Cambridge and was specially ordained at the hands of the Archbishop of Canterbury himself. By the time he was twenty-six he was not only a minor canon of St. Paul's but priest-in-ordinary to the king.

These brilliant successes of the young John Collins, steps up the ladder that would have delighted the most worldly and ambitious of prelates, are not only amusingly incongruous with most people's idea of the man, but show conclusively that his later role as a rebel or leader of protest came to him as a result of living experience and the convictions it brought, not at all from nature or from any breath of failure or enviousness. Later John was often to be slandered as a communist or fellow traveller, yet in the 'thirties when so many privileged young intellectuals were giving themselves to that faith, he was almost entirely happy as a good Anglican conservative – and serving in the Chapel Royal.

Before leaving this account of how John Collins reversed the common life line from idealistic and rebellious youth to sceptical and conforming age, I should like to carry it forward to the years after the war when he had already abandoned many of his old positions and could call himself a Christian socialist. He had indeed begun to exercise his moral muscle against unwise authority, having been four times threatened with court martial during his remarkable activities as an R.A.F. chaplain, as well as having already launched the great creative side of his ministry in founding Christian Action. To all this I shall return, but the years 1947–49 have a special relevance to my present theme. They were years of decisions that very largely shaped all that was to follow.

The central issue was the familiar one that confronts all those who want to change their society in any degree, from bloody revolution to the prevention of cruelty to animals; that is whether

Canon Collins baptizes his granddaughter in St. Paul's.

Above: Easter march from Aldermaston to London. (Left to right: Ritchie Calder, George Macleod, Canon Collins, Kingsley Martin, Jacquetta Hawkes, James Cameron and John Horner.)

Below: Demonstrators outside South Africa House in London demand the release of political prisoners in South Africa.

Sleeping rough in London.

The Easter Aldermaston march ends in Trafalgar Square.

Above: Inside a Christian Action hostel for homeless women.

Below: Demonstration in support of Treason Trial victims in South Africa.

Above : Paul Robeson at the lectern in St. Paul's.

Below : President Eisenhower signs the Roll of Honour for the American Memorial Chapel. (Left to right: Harold MacMillan, Canon Collins, President Eisenhower, Bishop Wand, Minor Canon Joseph Robinson and Head Verger Vernon Ovrington.)

Canon Collins, Michael Foot and Donald Soper leave 10 Downing Street after handing in a letter seeking British renunciation of nuclear weapons.

Above : Canon Collins talks with the Chairman of the Anti-Apartheid Sub-Committee at the United Nations.

Below : Bantu education.

to work from inside the established centres of power, a choice that involves at least some preliminary conformity and may end in self-betrayal, or whether to remain an unsullied outsider with no immediate power and the likelihood of ending with nothing more than clean hands and spiritual pride. On the other hand, of course, both offer the possibilities of success: within the present context insider or outsider could end as an Archbishop Temple or a Gandhi.

John Collins's first decision was a clear-cut one to avoid the toils that the upper Anglican management tried to cast round this dangerous fish that had appeared in their waters. He refused an invitation from Archbishop Fisher to become Secretary of the British Council of Churches. Then the following year, in 1948, he was offered a canonry at St. Paul's with the vigorous support of Sir Stafford Cripps, who saw this as the perfect base for the development of Christian Action into a great national movement of Christian regeneration. Now at this time, as John has told us in his autobiography, his whole upbringing and nature made him inclined to remain an insider. 'In fact,' he says, 'I was still naïve enough to suppose that the establishment could be stormed and redeemed from within itself.' So there, near the middle of his life, he was still so little an aggressive rebel at heart, that he went voluntarily – though not meekly – into that great stronghold of Anglicanism, St. Paul's. He even admits that he probably still cherished the normal ambition to become a bishop, which must then have appeared certain of early fulfilment.

Critics on one extreme might say that in opting for St. Paul's there had to be too much compromise, while those on the other would say that having made the choice it was unsuitable at once to draw red rags before high ecclesiastical noses. In judging the situation there must be an analogy with social democracy and a mixed economy. Does it yield the best of both worlds or the worst? My own judgement is that when enough time has passed for the whole picture to emerge it will be seen that John took the better decision and that even if the establishment withdrew its favours and often frustrated him, he was able to do much good as a part-time outsider working from the inside. However, the point here is to show how far the acceptance of the canonry and the devotion with which he has fulfilled the resulting duties (hence the 'part-time') finally disprove the notion that John Collins is a fanatic or born rebel.

With that mistake (I hope) disposed of, it is time to examine John's career as a leader of protests, and the attitudes and values that have inspired it. As a preliminary it is worth trying to isolate one or two principles or convictions that seem to have guided him in all that he has done. I say 'one or two' with intent, for at first there seemed to be two, but with thought I understood that one led so directly into the other that they could hardly be divided. The thing that first struck me is that in all his efforts to change society for the better he has been aiming towards some positive goal, and has not wanted to provoke but to achieve. It can truthfully be said that he has often been more protested against than protesting. Over the past decade protest has begun to sound like a dirty word in the ears of many of us who are by no means conformists. It has been corrupted by those who hardly seem to live unless they have a hostile placard in their hands and whose cause is little more than dislike of all authority. John's approach has always been from the opposite direction. He believes in living example and in fellowship through working together for particular purposes – whether these are to remove some abuse or to develop some good.

The second element within the governing principles is represented by this word 'particular'. John Collins is at one with William Blake in thinking that good must be done in 'Minute Particulars', the adjective being used in its sense of precise rather than small. He might not fully share the vehemence of the poet's declaration that 'General Good is the plea of the scoundrel, hypocrite and flatterer' but he would certainly agree that it expresses a truth in associating the general good with hypocrisy or self-deception. It is one of the sad truths that he has learned through experience. If, for example, he preached of brotherhood and love, the congregation would be happy, but when he particularized it to denouncing apartheid some would rise and stomp out; if he preached reconciliation his listeners would purr, but when he suggested this might mean the forgiveness of German war criminals they would arch their backs and spit.

Obviously, indeed, it is because he has kept to his faith in action for precise objectives that John has met with so much opposition in the world at large and within the Anglican establishment most of all. There are a number of Anglican priests who have been glad to be known as progressives and even leftists but whose careers have flourished like the green bay tree with no favours withheld.

They have as a rule kept safely within the bounds of 'General Good'.

Positive actions and particularity, then, are the maxims John Collins has followed in his march from almost unquestioning conformity to a position where he has had to work very largely as an outsider.

His questioning in fact began not over Christian involvement in social reform but over theological issues. An intelligent schoolboy's doubts about the fundamentalist view of scriptures and dogmas were lulled by the modernism he encountered at Cambridge. His experiences as a parish curate, when he found himself ill-prepared for ministering in the everyday world and found moreover that church society formed a small, closed circle remote from the majority of the people, were beginning to trouble him, but he was whisked back to Cambridge before such doubts had time to sprout. However, his capacity as a doubter and questioner soon showed itself again when his interest in the modernist movement of the Roman Church led to a strange friendship with Alfred Loisy who had been one of its leaders. Loisy's efforts to harmonize biblical exegesis with the findings of a scientific age had long before ended in his unfrocking as a heretic and 'agent of Satan'. John Collins went regularly to visit the old man in his French retreat – and that during a period when his own worldly prospects were at their most glittering.

During their last meeting the ex-priest told him, 'I have repudiated not Christianity, nor the church, but the obscurantism and intransigence of those who control and administer the church; and those who control and administer the church have repudiated me: so be it'.

During these years John's active exploration of the corridors of doubt was mainly of a theological kind because he was living in the sheltered precincts of academe. Yet as the 'thirties went by with their unemployment and hunger marches, their fascist take-overs and the brutalities of the Abyssinian and Spanish wars, the walls of Westcott House and Oriel could not protect so sensitive a conscience and heart as John's from penetration and response. He became more and more convinced that the church must involve itself in social and therefore in political affairs, less and less trustful of Tory Anglicanism and the establishment. Inevitably he saw his ideas for Christian participation linked with socialism and his best hope for socialism in the Labour Party.

This was a deep change of heart and of allegiances. It brought him new friends on the left, outstanding among them Stafford Cripps and Victor Gollancz, both men who had long been committed to bringing a religiously inspired morality into politics. Yet until 1940 the conversation remained not so much theoretical as inward. It had not been made manifest in action, for John's personal labours were still bent on preparing a commentary on the Acts of the Apostles. Not that this work was remote from what was to follow. The choice of subject was determined by his absorption in the idea of the dedicated spiritual group or 'cell' and the power it could generate.

The crack-up of war brought the advance from thought and feeling to action. It was in the uniform of an R.A.F. squadron-leader that John first became a well placed thorn in the flesh of the establishment. Again, however, I think it is true to say that as chaplain he did not set out to torment or rebel, but to make Christianity, and Anglican Christianity at that, come to full life within the community in which he found himself: the Training Command camp at Yatesbury; not that he was incapable of enjoying himself and a new sense of power when he found what a thorn he could be.

Looking ahead to the important roles John was to play on national and international stages, it may seem extravagant to give space to the fellowship he created at Yatesbury. Yet it would be mistaken, for there in microcosm were the characteristics that were to appear in later and greater ventures.

The first was his own deep Christian commitment. Those of us among his friends who do not have that commitment must never forget that it has always inspired his thinking and controlled his doing. Second was his determination not to work from above but from the roots upwards. The fellowship that was to become so renowned that its file reached the Prime Minister's desk, began as a tiny group of 'ordinary' airmen and airwomen. In this I think John has differed sharply from Cripps, Gollancz and other eminences who have worked with him. Then again there was the astuteness linked with moral courage that John discovered in himself. They were evoked when the side of the fellowship's programme that expressed the Christian's duty to be involved in 'social, economic and political affairs' brought him into collision with higher authority in both air force and church.

As I have already suggested to be typical of John, he began with positive aims, and the element of protest grew only when these were, as he saw it, improperly frustrated. In this case the protest was in effect against the official view (quite outside King's Regulations which he took care never to break) that service personnel should be insulated from all controversial political activities. When the fellowship was responsible for inviting Cripps and 'the red dean' of Canterbury into the bosom of the camp to lecture, an attempt was made to keep them out. John refused to cancel the lectures, was summoned before the C-in-C Training Command and won the day by showing that he had not infringed Regulations and that the C-in-C had no authority over him in his priestly capacity. The overlord gave way – but amended the rules to the effect that no further lectures should be arranged without his permission. The point of telling this story here lies in a sequel which illustrates John Collins's growing political astuteness. When the camp, like the world outside, was tense with feeling about the Russians' demand for a second front, the fellowship, by now a powerful influence, decided to arrange visits by representatives of Allied governments in London, including the Russian ambassador. It was obvious that Mr. Maisky would not be welcome in an R.A.F. camp, but John saw at once how the emended regulations could be used to put the responsibility for denying his visit on to the authorities, so exposing the pretence of trust in our great, red ally. He simply invited Mr. Maisky to come, warning him that permission had to be given by the C-in-C.

Diplomatic embarrassment over a refusal carried this affair up and up until Churchill himself intervened, minuting that the chaplain at Yatesbury must be either a communist or a dupe – the first of many such accusations.

In the Maisky affair John received his blooding as a leader of resistance. He must also have felt his own strength and recognized the occasional vulnerability of the establishment. The last phase of the war further hardened his attitude. The saturation bombing of Germany capped by the final horror of Hiroshima and Nagasaki had two effects. They made him very nearly a total pacifist, although – another proof of his native moderation – he has never been prepared to deny 'the use of force in any and every circumstance'. Secondly, the total failure of the church to give any lead in this moral crisis of mankind must greatly have intensified his conviction, already proclaimed through the fellowship, that such evasiveness or dullness of spirit could only end in death and that

Christians must go out into the world to inspire and, where necessary, to protest.

From this point John Collins's fulfilment of his resolve will be described in other sections of our book. All I can properly do here is to examine some signposts along the way of protest.

It is now quite hard to believe that Christian Action started with the full backing of such establishment figures as Lord Halifax and that it came near to being an anti-communist movement. Although 'particularity' in the form of a drive for the repatriation of German prisoners-of-war provoked some disapproval, it long basked in general goodwill. The first turning-point came in 1952 when Christian Action advanced from an acceptable concern for race relations in South Africa to open support for the Defiance campaign of the African National Congress. Now for the first time in his career John was involved with illegal action, albeit in a far country. Moreover he used the pulpit of St. Paul's to denounce Dr. Malan and apartheid. (In thinking of John as a protester one must always remember the fearless use he has made of preaching. In sermon after sermon he has made action explicit in words.)

Lord Halifax politely resigned from Christian Action, the Archbishops of Canterbury and Westminster both withdrew their representatives: the movement and its creator were no longer respectable. The dream of storming and redeeming the establishment from within had dissolved.

John was quite unrepentant, and soon a visit to South Africa convinced him even more deeply of the evils of apartheid and the duty of Christian resistance to it. Already he was a marked man and on his arrival in Durban saw posters screaming 'Collins Go Home'. It is revealing that he could not at first think to whom they were addressed. Now completely involved in the train of history – with the Treason Trial, Sharpeville and their sequels – it was impossible to resist the pressure of events. Christian Action tried for a time to withhold support from any form of violence, but when the ANC was forced by internal politics to move from passive resistance to acts of sabotage and some of its finest leaders were arrested and faced with the death penalty, Christian Action abandoned its scruples and came to their defence.

Probably quite a few friends of John and of Christian Action regretted that this last turning-point had to be passed and violence condoned. No one has given the problem more thought than John himself, and he has come to the moderate conclusion that in spite of self-multiplying evils of violence and its incompatibility with the gospel of love, we should not withhold 'our sympathy from those who, deprived of their political freedom and having lost confidence in non-violent resistance, turn to violence'.

CND in which John was simultaneously involved proved his refusal to condone not only violence but passive law-breaking in a free society. Like the rest of the leadership, he never allowed the Campaign itself to be involved in such activities, when in later years they were urged by all manner of silly, frustrated or bloody-minded persons and factions. On the great Aldermaston marches, I can bear witness to the easy correctness of his dealings with the police, always wishing to help them keep good order, but implacable when he felt they were exceeding their powers in diverting and dividing the marchers.

Undoubtedly CND brought John his apotheosis as a man of protest and resistance. Here for the first time there was no general Christian involvement but, as Mervyn Jones so well shows, a bringing together of the most extraordinary medley of people united and inspired by their total opposition to an insane evil. Moreover he was able to cleave to his leading convictions. There was the particularity of nuclear disarmament adhered to in spite of all efforts to broaden our objectives towards General Good, there was a vast amount of energy coming from below, there was a blend of intelligence with feeling, and for a long time there was at the heart of the Campaign a bond of friendship and of spreading personal relationships. So although this was wholly a movement of protest, it was during its rise protest with a joyous face.

This is not the place to weigh the successes and failures of John's long effort to change the worse for the better. Nor has it been possible to set it as clearly as I should have liked in the whole historical context of its period. CND, obviously, even more than John's other activities, belonged to and fanned a mounting gale of protest affecting everything from the length of young men's hair to the greatest questions of our national life. Many, even of those of us who furthered it, may now feel that the time has come to begin (if we can) a shift from protest to reconstruction, from a romantic to a classic mood.

Whatever happens, and whatever judgement the future may make, I feel confident that another generation will recognize how fortunate it was that John Collins was among the leaders through those days of change. He sacrificed much to bring his own faith and values into movements that might otherwise have been destructive and hate-filled. He has always believed 'By their fruits you shall know them'. He will come out well from that test.

PART FOUR

ACTION IN REFLECTION

1 THE INTUITION OF UNITY IN MORALS

Iris Murdoch

The idea of unity or unification is one of the fundamental ideas of philosophy, and also of science. It is one of the fundamental ideas of human nature. Western philosophy begins when Plato becomes obsessively puzzled by the fact that although we only experience what is fragmentary and imperfect yet we seem to know about what is whole and perfect. This too was the problem of Hume, Kant and Hegel. We see parts of things but we intuit or believe in whole things. We experience bad conduct but we know about good conduct. We take it that we ourselves are unities: a single body, a single mind. We grasp space and time as continuous and somehow unitary. We perceive and can deal with all kinds of other assumed unities: nation states, works of art, theories, human history itself.

Of the philosophers who made this their chief concern the most truly sceptical was Hume, who was prepared to say that these unities were actually illusions; the self, the material object – illusions. Hume himself admitted that the idea was repugnant to common sense and his greatest critic, Kant, found it unbearable. The urge to show that where we intuit unity there is in some sense really unity is one of the deepest motives to philosophy. Intellect itself is naturally one-making, and it is tempting to suppose that mind and reality mirror each other. To evaluate or understand anything, to prefer or classify, implies some degree of unified system. The questing mind abhors vacuums and lacunae. A whole philosophy, Hegelian idealism, rests upon this idea.

We seek to connect and unify our surroundings primarily as a matter of instinct and the need to survive. A grasp of causality, for instance, is essential to a practising human being. Philosophical explanations of this 'instinct' are of course various. We also unify for secondary and less compulsory theoretical reasons, for instance in pursuit of truth. Science creates unifying notations to express deep similarities of structure. There are other motives for unification which are neither compulsory nor entirely rational. We unify data for aesthetic reasons. A harmonious pattern pleases the mind and prompts memory. Authorities and institutions unify and simplify in order to persuade and control. We unify for comfort and consolation, because to unify data is a source of energy and an exercise of power, and because a scattered accidental world is frightening and horrible and we wish to transform horror into history or tragedy or science.

I shall take several related cases where this intuitive unification which goes beyond the given data takes place. Many philosophers have started similar quests by considering our concept of a *thing*. It is remarkable that whereas we seem to perceive only parts of things under ephemeral conditions of perspective, light and so on, we yet firmly believe in the existence of persisting material objects of steadfast shape and uniform colour. The material object or thing also provides us with our instinctive paradigm for many other kinds of unity, including some quite dissimilar ones. I am not however going to talk about things. I want to start with the case of a work of art. A work of art is of course not a material object. Some works of art are bodied forth by material objects and may seem to inhere in them more or less remotely. In the case of a statue the relation between the material object and the art object seems very close, in the case of a picture less close. No one is tempted to imagine that poems or symphonies are material objects, though we need objects, such as books, in order to get at them. Some art objects need to be performed by secondary artists in order to be perceived by their clients. Others need only to be more or less strenuously 'performed' by the client or consumer himself. What exactly a work of art is remains a difficult philosophical problem: I suggest as a working hypothesis that a work of art is an ideal unity or quasi-thing which we imaginatively 'compose', retain in the attention, and enjoy through a joint activity of our intellect and senses, construing it upon the paradigm of a material thing. Although it is not 'perceptible' in the ordinary sense, its accessibility depends upon a fairly precise and fixed sensory notation or 'body'. Looking at the paint is not looking at the picture, nor is hearing sounds hearing a symphony. We have to see *as* a picture, hear *as* a symphony. On the other hand, the symphony does not exist simply in the hearer's mind. It has an external being and an external authority to which the hearer submits himself.

It is interesting that the rather sophisticated idea of an art object is one which people in our civilization seem able to acquire so easily. (Even understanding two dimensions as three is a skill not possessed by all human beings.) From nursery days when we are invited to admire pictures and listen to stories we grasp roughly how we are meant to enjoy such things. We learn the word 'beauty' and how the beautiful is something separate and special which we look at. We also readily discern beauty in both art and nature, although the characteristics of the two areas are so different.

The work of art has attracted the attention of philosophers, though somewhat intermittently. Hegelian idealism idolizes the peculiar mentally sustained organic unity of the art object and uses it not only as a paradigm but as a touchstone: the more highly organized the more real. Anglo-Saxon empiricists have never bothered much about art, and it is perhaps significant that the aesthetic problem which mainly interests them at present is not the old respectable question of what makes a good work of art, but the more 'logical' question of what makes a work of art at all, what is its definition. This shift of interest is symptomatic of a more critical, less idolatrous attitude to art which is characteristic of the present day. In some quarters art and the art object are actually under attack. The motives for this attack are understandable and in many ways decent. It is felt that European art has become too grand and out of touch. The mood of existentialism favoured sincere expression of feeling rather than meticulous statement, and the mood of utilitarianism finds the artificiality of art frivolous in a menaced and suffering world. This discontent finds expression among artists in the cult of the ephemeral or of the shockingly incomplete. Art provokes its client. Pictures leave their frames, ordinary artefacts or natural objects are exhibited as if they were works of art, and audiences are expected to invent their own theatre.

The idealist philosophers used the work of art as a paradigm and as a touchstone, and I shall do so too, in a different way. The objective is in fact the idea of goodness, not the idea of art, but a consideration of art and the art object will make it easier to state certain things about morality. I want to suggest in more detail why works of art are so important to us, and why they are important even to those who reject them, since the attack on art is partly homage to art too, whether it comes from artists or from dictators. I shall put this study in terms of: the case for art, and the case against art.

The case for art inspires a prompt eloquence. Art is both informative and entertaining, but this alone does not explain our veneration for it. Art informs and entertains in a particular way. It condenses and clarifies the world so as to direct our attention upon particular things. This intense showing or demonstration of which it is capable is detested by tyrants, who always persecute or demoralize their artists. Art overcomes the strict causality and accident which makes ordinary life such a senseless muddle, and enables us to survey complex or horrible things which would otherwise baffle or frighten us. Art creates an authoritative public human world, a treasury of past experience which resists change. It gives us energy by purifying and unifying our feelings. In enjoying great art we experience a clarification and perfection of our own consciousness. Art is the taking-off place of intuitions of ideal formal and symbolic unity which enables us to co-operate with the artist and be, as we enjoy the work, artists ourselves. The art object presents to us the idea of a transcendent unsullied beyond, a permanent untouchable reality not soiled by contingency or base calculating human motive. Great art inspires us because it is separate, it is for nothing, it is for itself. Its clarified symbolism enables us to look without sin upon a sinful world. It renders innocent and transforms into a mode of truthful vision our baser energies connected with power, curiosity, envy, and sex.

So might run a statement in praise of art. But turn now to the opposing case. Here it may be said at once: yes indeed, the argument for art is really the argument against art, and one need hardly say more. One has only to explain clearly what art is and what it does in order to see what is wrong with it. This idolization of art depends upon an unexamined idea of perfection. These so-called ideal unities are really illusory unities. Art is fake objects producing fake consciousness, and blurring the possibility of real honesty and truthful understanding. Art is consolation offered instead of truth. It may be said that only bad art thus misleads; but is not almost all art bad? And even 'good art' is very largely magic, illusion. The greatest of all thinkers, Plato, was an enemy of art and excluded the poets from the ideal state. Let us consider why. Why indeed did Plato not take the art object as the image of the good (as Hegel did)? The work of art, transcendent, clarified, explanatory, unsoiled by the world, shedding light upon the miserable human scene, prompting compassion and understanding, seems the very image of goodness itself: a sort of semi-sensory image of a spiritual good, a concrete universal, and something in fact very like a Platonic 'Idea' or 'Form'.

Plato pictures the spiritual life as a progressive clarification, a movement towards selfless lucidity taking place under the inspiration of ideas of perfection. The Platonic Forms are creative, they are sources of energy, divine entities which the soul has seen before birth and now vaguely remembers. Most memorable and most accessible to incarnate beings is beauty (we learn in the *Phaedrus*); but Plato means natural beauty, not the 'beauty' of art. In fact he uses sexual love as an example and speaks of the beauty of the lovely boy whom the lover reveres as a god. Plato does not value the 'superficial charms' of natural scenery; he regards as spiritual purgation the search for truth in philosophy and (as a path thereto) the study of mathematics and cosmic natural laws and the enjoyment of these as beautiful. Even the exercise of a humble craft is a discovery of necessary structure and a revelation of the beauty of the world.

Plato rejects art as a source of moral inspiration because it is too closely linked to the strong self-directed self-deceiving forces of the mind. Art rejects reality and necessity, and produces instead a consoling untruthful picture of the world where, in the interests of a false 'beauty', causality has been conveniently altered to suit the dreaming ego. Art is essentially motivated by and caters for the lower part of the soul, as we are told at the end of the *Republic*. The artist is not interested in studying or commending goodness, which is lucid and quiet; even when he pretends to criticize it, he celebrates evil and makes it fascinating and attractive. The charm of art induces the nobler part of the mind to 'relax its guard' (Plato's phrase), so that we are able to indulge secretly in shameful emotions. Art enchants us into envisaging and being infected by cruelty, depravity and spite which we would otherwise reject and shun. While thus corrupting us, art often appears to offer a genuine commentary on human affairs, and apes a sort of insight, a simplicity which in its true form is a spiritual achievement. We intuit in art a perfection and a truth which are not really there.

The relevance of Plato's view to the present day hardly needs emphasis. Television is the very image of life in the cave. He gives a reasoned expression to the attitudes both of the social watchdogs

117

who think art is corrupting and of the anti-art artists who think that it is insincere. Freud (who several times declares himself a Platonist and tells us that his *libido* is Plato's *eros*) holds an essentially similar view of art. His main thesis, variously expressed, is that art is the fantasy life of the artist stimulating the fantasy life of his client, with the work of art lying half abandoned in between as a sort of disguise or bribe. As Freud explains (in *The Poet and Day Dreaming: Collected Papers*, vol. 4) we would normally be repelled by the private fantasies of another person, but the artist persuades us to accept his by disguising them cleverly and by offering us purely formal and aesthetic pleasures which then incite us to release, on our side, a play of fantasy which is normally inhibited. 'The true enjoyment of literature proceeds from the release of tensions in our minds. Perhaps much that brings about this result consists in the writer putting us into a position in which we can enjoy our day dreams without reproach or shame.'

What on this view becomes of the dignity and innocence of the work of art? The ideal unity which we imagine that we experience is seen to be an illusory unity indeed; or rather, the unity which we intuit is not what we think it is. Art is not the creation of clarified unified public objects, it is the production of maimed pseudo-objects which are licenses for the private concluding processes of personal fantasy. The sense of power which the contemplation of such objects inspires in us is then easily explained; and we can understand too our peculiar delight in the condensed symbolism of poetry and painting, concerning which recent criticism has so often taken pleasure in vindicating Freud's theory of the hidden bribe.

Let it be said here by way of transition that, in my opinion, Plato's and Freud's criticisms are partly just; and it is their insight in this field which I now want to transfer bodily to another field. Roughly: Plato did not take the art object as the paradigm of good for certain reasons. For the same reasons one cannot take Good as the paradigm of good. The nature of the illusory unity is the same in each case. The idea of a perfect and transcendent Good has of course been most familiar to us in the form of a perfect and transcendent God. I wish to argue that the power and fascination of this now much criticized object have occasioned one of those regularly occurring false dichotomies in philosophy. Important ethical ideas have become attached by a natural attraction to this powerful unity and have been wrongly rejected with it, leaving the field free for individualistic behaviourist theories of will which depend on the rejection of any definition of good, or for sociological utilitarianism. Ideas about beauty and virtue, high quality of consciousness and high quality of happiness, since they seemed inseparable from this sort of theological aesthetic, have been abandoned in a general rejection of metaphysics by an age of science.

A personal God felicitously combines the characteristics of an art object and of a philosophical idea with those of an ideal creator-cum-spectator. Here the satisfying unification of our feelings takes place by being observed more than through observing. God is the guarantor of the real unified existence of the individual as responsible, as morally judged, perhaps as able to survive death. What corresponds here to our pleasure in art is an invigorating sense of guilt connected with a corresponding sense of innocence and possible salvation. Strict causality and the contingent aspects of time are thus ideally overcome, in our own case and by extension in that of others; so that, as in tragedy, we can survey the misery of the world more calmly. In so far as our religion provides us with a mythology, a story, characters, images, pictures, it is of course in itself a sort of work of art. Religious imagery colours and fixes and bodies forth certain moral ideas. This is particularly so in the case of Christianity, whose centre is so essentially one special, marvellously narrated story. Christ as *Logos* is the God of the philosophers, the ultimate unifying principle, the guarantor of reason and science. Christ as Redeemer is the perfect (beautiful, aesthetic) image of how the ordinary man is saved from everything that he fears most; there is the blotting out of sins, the triumph of suffering over death, the substitution of punishment for death. Even the idea of a just judgement, *cum vix iustus sit securus*, is a profound comfort, unless one is quite certain one is damned. And of course God also performs another of the tasks performed by the work of art, in making sex seem innocent. The Greeks were fairly detached about their gods. Aristotle even found the idea of loving God absurd. But Jews and Christians take God as the supreme love-object; and it is one of the most profound and attractive elements of their faith that impure feelings are supposed to be purified by being directed upon a pure object.

It is easy to picture the good in terms of the more favourable and comforting idea of the work of art. I want now to deploy in a new context 'the case against art', and to do this by relating the ideas of good and art to the idea of individual or self. The essence of Freud's case, and also of Plato's, is that art stimulates private self-activity; so that the enjoyment of art is not what it seems.

Let us consider this self-activity, its nature and its needs. Plato, like Freud, is concerned with the division of the self into parts and the relation of these parts to different levels of reality; and the Hegelians and Marxists are also of course in this respect Platonists, the enlightening self-clarification being the work of divine logic or history. Since Descartes however western philosophers have been generally less concerned about levels of illusion, and more concerned about the unity and identity of the self as a whole. Hume attempted a radical scepticism, presenting the self as a bundle of perceptions unified by powerful habits of imagination. Kant invented a complex knower who *had* to exist as the necessary counterpart of indubitably known truths of science. Modern philosophy has again attempted scepticism. (It is never all that easy to be a sceptic.) Both Sartre and Wittgenstein have attacked the idea of the self as a continuous substantial entity and as the privileged knower of private truths. Piecemeal psychological and sociological studies of personality begin to take the whole subject away from traditional philosophy. This dwindling or disappearance of 'the self', coinciding with the fading of religious belief in the soul, prompts and supports a behaviouristic ethics which emphasizes will and rules as aspects of action, rather than virtue and pureness of heart as aspects of consciousness.

One does not need to be a philosopher to grasp the problem and the drama of the self; and the philosopher leaving his study will no sooner doubt the existence of the things that surround him than the existence of himself. In fact, 'thing' and 'self' may seem to be guarantors of each other, not only philosophically but psychologically: we are reassured about our own continued existence by the continued existence of our familiar surroundings. And again that we sometimes need reassurance is something which we do not have to be told by a theory. We are at once powerfully persuaded that we exist, and profoundly frightened lest we should cease to exist, as continuous beings. Anything which fragments consciousness, such as an inability to remember or to assemble appearances, produces fear: the suspicion that the ego is not the one all-powerful unifier which it would like to be. This is perhaps the deepest reason why the ideas of the art object and of the single transcendent good, philosophical or religious, have been so much prized.

The art object and the single good are powerful unifiers of the self, and also prime images and analogies of the self. These represent exactly what the self, with its deepest instincts, would like to be: secure, timeless, unified and unmocked.

Thus by taking seriously the case against art, and by relating and assimilating to each other art object, good and self, we seem to be moving by another route towards the sceptical position of modern philosophy concerning the philosophical idea of the substantial self. As between the cases of self, art and good, there is of course a difference of status, since it is the activity of the self which lends an air of spurious unity to art and good, while these in turn are taken back into the self in a degraded form as patterns of an illusory selfhood. That the idea of God is employed in this way was of course suggested by Hegel and Marx; and modern thought which attacks the self also attacks good, God and even art. Yet at this point of apparent agreement it may be doubted whether modern philosophy is really quite as sceptical or as empiricist as it seems. Philosophy has rejected the old metaphysical unities. Even the idea of a single faculty of reason is now rejected by most western philosophers. Philosophy appears to favour multiplicity rather than unity. Yet where the central problem of common consciousness and human mode of being is concerned, the disappearance of the old substantial self has not meant the realistic acceptance of an active, more disunited self, but rather the continuance of other metaphysical ideas of tinier deprived but still unitary selflets, leading a minimal yet dignified existence as principles of will or sincerity or non-universal reason. That is, the idea of the single pure entity which somehow defines or constitutes the self has not really been surrendered after all. Philosophers have wanted to retain some semblance of this free directing sovereign, rather than letting it descend into the disunited stuff of a more empirically conceived consciousness. At the same time, this natural ordinary daily *activity* of self-life, because it was reflected in an illusory manner in the great metaphysical unities, has been set aside with them, and the self as a mode of being, a sort of material or quality of moment-to-moment consciousness, has on the whole been abandoned by philosophy as if this idea were itself a mistake. The study of the self as an active illusionist living in a world of appearance and reality has been handed over to science, while inside philosophy the problem is 'solved' by some variant of a metaphysic of will. This reductionism limits the concepts available to moral philosophy, since there is no clarified vocabulary in which the quality of consciousness can be described, and no place where the relation of morality to ordinary self-being can be regularly discussed.

I want to argue that the self, our personal consciousness or mode of being, is the seat of a radical incompleteness which is our individual view of the incompleteness of everything. (As Plato puts it, human affairs are not serious but have to be taken seriously.) The 'rescue' of this concept by metaphysical philosophy is not surprising if one considers the deep escapist purposes of the ego. Without the defence of 'system' the self is seen as subject to a miserable degree of contingency; and most modern philosophers (not the later Wittgenstein) are in a modest way system-makers. The unprotected self which, separated from the false unities which enclosed it, can now be studied, is not a philosophical subject designed to solve a philosophical problem. It is the obscure entity that we somehow know that we are, the place where we live, our extended yet interrupted worm of consciousness which is so familiar and yet so puzzling. The self is its consciousness and yet it is more than its consciousness, and just in that 'more than' it is so hard to escape illusion. Few philosophers have really tried to describe self-being and perhaps none has done so without an ulterior systematic purpose. The self which Hume describes is largely a philosophical invention. Sartre (in *L'Etre et le Néant*) describes one aspect of consciousness very vividly; his sharp distinction between inert and vacuous mind precludes a more detailed investigation. (For him, as for Kant, mind is either stuff or freedom, and the stuff is roughly all of one sort.) Wittgenstein sometimes suggests what active consciousness is like, but always in a discussion of concepts of quite other kinds.

The self, whether as immediate consciousness or as extended self-being, is notoriously hard to describe. The efforts made by novelists exhibit some of the problems involved. The self is not like an ordinary empirical object. It is difficult to characterize it justly at all without using some kind of evaluative or highly toned language. This is certainly one reason for the uneasiness, where this entity is concerned, of philosophers who wish to make a clear distinction between factual and evaluative discourse. Philosophers in the past who did not make this distinction often argued from the nature of the soul, as they took it in reality to be, to the nature of the good (emphasizing for these purposes the soul as unifier and system-maker). I think that however lucidly one tries to talk about the mystery of human consciousness it is impossible to avoid moral implications of some kind. This may be regarded as a reason for not talking, or as part of an argument for ethical naturalism. I think that morality is connected with self-nature and is indeed grounded in it. But I am suggesting an emphasis which is the reverse of the traditional one. Roughly: it is not the self as system-maker, but the self as overcoming illusions of system that is the spring of virtue. (Kant's Reason destroys systems, but is itself a System.) This is the natural human task which is a fundamental form of morality. What really transcends the self is not its own glorified and unified self-image, but the world, more formless and broken and horrible, and also more beautiful, than is pictured in the mediocre unifying 'art' of our usual imaginings. This is an idea which it is perhaps easier for us to grasp now than ever before, since science has cracked the theoretical and aesthetic unities of metaphysics and religion and destroyed any imaginable picture of the cosmos.

I do not here embark upon the study or description of self-being for which I have been trying to make a philosophical place. Some of its essentials have been stated. The self is a mechanism which instinctively protects itself by illusions, some private to the individual, others belonging to groups or societies. Often the protection consists in attributing unity and secure being to what is in reality fragmentary and insecure. The self pictures itself as complete, powerful, attractive and unmockable. If it can, it furnishes its world with secure unified entities: God, the state, history, works of art. There are philosophical reasons for regarding such intuitions of unity as misleading. Psychoanalysis also breaks down false self-pictures in so far as these constitute neuroses which damage the efficiency of the ego, and we can learn much from analytical theory about the mechanism of the psyche. Analysis however is therapy, not morality, and is presumably content to leave unimpaired and even to promote the self-unity of the healthy ego. What I am saying implies that even the healthy ego is likely to be making a sort of mistake. In saying this I move over the border of ordinary empirical talk into a kind of talk which can only characterize its subject matter in a morally coloured way. In fact moral philosophers cannot be neutral and had better not pretend to be. What is required is clarity about the values which one is discussing and presenting (recommending). Common sense constantly notes the disunity of its world and then forgets it again. It is the work of an exceptional being to be able to accept fundamental disunity and live with it and draw energy from it: to accept a random unmetaphysical mortal world not even saved by love. I have been implying that this acceptance is a deep form and source of goodness: that goodness is virtue in the sense of an unillusioned quality of consciousness. This is of course a moral judgement, and a philosophical idea which can be only very inconclusively argued. Part of the argument consists in the foregoing criticism of illusions of unity, the analogy between the self and the art object, and between the self and the false idea of a unified transcendent good. Another part of the argument would consist of descriptions of moral activity, showing how what we recognize as goodness is connected with the overcoming of natural egocentric duplicity, and how morally good actions spring from an acceptance of the world as multifarious and incomplete. Here an important exercise would be an examination of, for instance, religious faith so as to show that counterexamples were merely apparent.

At any rate it can be clear that a reduction in our expectations of unity (a unified self, a unified cosmos) means a serious reduction in our personal dignity. Humility is a name for this radical abandonment of dignity. The vision of the disconnected world which the ego so much dreads may be found to be a source of energy, even of happiness, when the protective illusions begin to vanish. The ego unifies and simplifies the world, as it unifies and simplifies the material object, in order to impose itself upon it. When the unifying force of this imposition is relaxed there is very much to be seen, including other people who are quite different from oneself; and to see the real is to see its claims. The removal of the metaphysical unities and of the curiously material paraphernalia of western religion clears the way for a sort of natural mysticism which has always been understood in the east. Deprived of false ideas of oneself and God as somehow deploying an elsewhere where all is perfected, one's grasp of one's present being is strengthened and one relies upon the immediate quality of this being to relate oneself to the world. A true sense of the present is also a sense of causality, a sense of limitation and accident, of how the quality of our being depends upon circumstance and history and is not easily amenable to change. An unillusioned self-consciousness is itself a sense of quality or grade of being, and the perception of our moral level, our subjection in this respect for causality, is in turn a source of strength. Our moral being springs out of the quality of our consciousness and this is its basis in nature.

A sense of quality of consciousness is also of course a sense of happiness or its absence. The shedding of illusions may cause fear or grief but is often for many people an obvious source of happiness. With the loss of absolute dignity, of the big unified protected ego, comes the loss of anxiety and envy and crude ambition. (This is a place for a definition of freedom.) A sense of fragmentariness may even be at least an exercise in overcoming the fear of death. We do not exist all that much, whatever instinct says. And since our salvation and that of others is not stored up for us anywhere else, we are stirred to work for a high quality of existence in the small area which we do possess. This could provide a natural basis for a new utilitarianism which could coexist with its respectable Benthamite counterpart. None of what I am saying denies our obvious practical need to live with and by rules and axioms, though my argument suggests that these configurations do not enter into the deep reality of what we are – they are not based upon the soul nor are they reflections of it. Political axioms, especially those which express and defend our liberal political world, are no doubt best thought of as isolated intuitions or rules, not professing to be based on general system and indeed resisting general system. Benthamite utilitarianism, and theories of natural rights which are related to it, rest upon such axioms. The obligation to relieve suffering does not depend upon a general view of goodness any more than it depends upon a general religious view. But it would be possible to develop behind Bentham's doctrine, not quite touching it and yet illuminating it, a utilitarianism concerned with quality of being and admitting in a sober way the idea of virtue as a kind of non-obsessive non-egoistic humility out of which good actions are likely to spring. As soon as we begin to overcome blinding self-obsession we tend to become happier ourselves and naturally to desire the happiness of others. This is not unlike Mill's view, only Mill was too subservient to Bentham's mode of argument to make the concept of virtue the centre of his theory. These two wings or aspects of utilitarianism, which may be called 'axiomatic utilitarianism' and 'natural utilitarianism' could enrich and clarify each other, though it would also be important that they be kept theoretically separate. The need, in a miserable world, to promote simple basic happiness, even mediocre and low-quality happiness, must never be made senseless by the existence of spiritual refinement, however natural (in a way) the latter may be.

After this excursion elsewhere let us return to the subject of art. I wish in conclusion to redeploy my main argument in relation to art, where I think it will show up more clearly and plainly, for properly understood art is still an image of morality after all. Our illusions about art and good are similar and throw light on one another. Perhaps now too we can put the case for art better, and produce an answer to the destructive critics. One must not expect too much of art, one must not deify it. On the other hand, it is a source of moral revelation. Bad art displays the bad aspects of human nature more clearly than anything else, though of course not so harmfully. (The exemplification of sin in bad art is a clearer warning to us than its *representation* in good art.) Bad art is moreover a sound producer of that low-quality happiness which Benthamite utilitarians might properly regard as a natural right. The art object as a false unity is an analogon of the self. The bad romantic story is the sentimental and untruthful account of how the brave attractive ego triumphs over accident and causality and is never really mocked or brought to nought. In fact it is very difficult for any artist not to falsify; the temptation to the ego is enormous, since it really does seem in this context to dispose of the godlike powers of which it has always dreamt. However, the good artist resists temptation and endeavours to tell the truth. Truth is always the proper touchstone in art, and a training in art is very largely a training in how to use the touchstone. Its use may be far from easy.

Art is artificial, an indirect truth-telling which delights in its own artifice. Perhaps we should not be too much troubled by theoretical problems about that fascinating western object, the work of art. Rightly, the art object is a kind of illusion, a false unity, but art can still communicate happiness and truth. Very few works of art, except for extremely simple ones, are really complete or free from gritty random elements. We the clients provide the illusion of smooth separateness and formal completion: the pseudo-object lives purified in our minds. Nevertheless in the hands of a great artist the object does not mislead; although thus 'complete' it proclaims incompleteness, and mirrors not the false unity of the self but its real disunity, its bafflement. Good art accepts and celebrates the defeat of the discursive intellect by the world. Bad art falsifies the world so as to pretend that there is no such defeat.

Comic art has an obvious delight in the absurd and a built-in principle of disunity too. Bad tragedy is solemn and cannot deal with the absurd without falling into bathos. Good tragedy continues to mock itself, internally, not by the factitious inclusion of comic elements: *King Lear*, a story of lost dignity, a supremely aesthetic display of a loss of aesthetic satisfaction. Lear plays bad tragedy in his mind, wanting to be consoled by dignity in defeat; but all collapses into senseless horror as in real defeats. In fact much of the greatest art is a sort of tragic-comic condensation which eschews definition and declared formal purpose: the great paintings, the great novels, *Henry IV*.

Looked at in this way we see that art, when it is good, has a beauty which is not so completely unlike the beauty of nature. It returns to the world, it opens vistas which are endless. Nature is, as it were, relentless causality made visible. Good art also displays an acceptance of causality. To accept causality, to refuse the consolation of false unities or false forms is also to accept one's own unavoidable present level and one's own unavoidable sort of being. As we enter into the awareness of the artist we begin to know ourselves and to live where we belong, inside our present consciousness. Art shows us what is true but usually invisible. Delight in natural beauty is a delight in the unfinished work of relentless causal forces. Art is only in a sense finished because it has to be. ('A poem is never finished, it is only abandoned.' Valéry.) But it expresses in an apparent object the mortality and savage incompleteness of things which we also contemplate in nature; and bodies forth what virtue springs from, a truthful sober vision of the world, presenting it to us half playfully as a source of moral energy and joy.

We can moreover perceive here the proper sense in which art is not just 'for itself' or 'for art's sake'. The independence of art is of course rightly emphasized in order to deny that it is essentially a social tool. Art has no 'social function', though artists do in fact usually serve their society in important ways, for instance by framing truths which could not otherwise be communicated. As against society, even as against a good society, art should be left free. But art, like morality, has its basis in nature, and has in fact the same basis. Equally, one emphasizes that morality must be free choice when one is resisting the dictatorship of institutions. (Freedom may be defined as 'axiomatic' or as 'natural'.) But neither morality nor art is 'free' in the sense of unconnected with human nature. This is one of those obvious truths for which it is so difficult to find a theoretical 'place'. Art arises out of the natural self-being of the psyche, and when we study that being we see what art is and what makes it good or bad; just as we see there what morality is and what makes conduct good or bad. This is the deep sense in which art can show us how good rests upon life; which is what so many philosophers have wanted to believe.

2 A TRIBUTE TO JOHN COLLINS ON HIS 70th BIRTHDAY

Raymond Kunene

Your progeny circles like two swallows
Feeding with both hands the exiled children.
By your wisdom we have built two neighbouring villages
And beautiful things come with your flowers of the night;
Your red baskets of early harvests scatter their abundance for the
      young bird.
From the cliff-edge the roar of your voices echoes into the ocean
Then the man-eater bird flees into the round nest of storms.
With its giant claw it threatens others
Running for shelter into your evenings.
By this camouflage she breeds the young of the lizard.
But you, who boast the clan of the Black Bird
You have warned the sun to close her eye of fruitfulness
To generate anger in those who are round-lipped like waterlilies.
A great feast comes with the birth of the sun.
The assembled crowds sing to the swallow's crescent wings.
Your face appears like a vision from ancient times
Emerging with the beams of light thrusting its scalpels of fire into
      the chasms of sleep.
You sing to the morning the pure anthem of the shepherd
Your song like a shield against time huddling the oasis.
You have raised your fingers to their lips with water
Touching them with drops of water.
By this sacred act each eye glistens with fire.
Every breast of truthfulness bears its children
Like hosts of butterflies disturbed from their tropical home.
I saw your arms flung against their night like streaks of lightning!
I heard your echoes of friendliness like peals of thunder
You planted the green mushrooms in the bowels of a cave

To be reaped in the quiet season
Like the moonflower that is born a thousand years in secret,
To feed and nourish each new generation with the ancestral dream.
There are those who come with every season
Whose vision bursts into the wombs of the universe
Like time-infinite, their cycles, like the twilight children of the sun!

KEY TO SYMBOLISM

1. Swallows in Africa are associated with the season of plenty. Many rulers whose era is regarded as historically significant are referred to as 'the black swallow that brought the harvest'. The swallow's crescent wings are seen in relation to the half moon that is believed to initiate a new rich season.
2. To give with both hands is customary among African people. It symbolizes the act of giving with one's whole heart. It also describes the unity between the two peoples, i.e. the givers and the receivers.
3. The night is regarded as potent, a period in which things grow. Like the black (fertile) soil it evokes associates with an earth that is rich. Hence 'the flowers of the night' are flowers that are particularly extravagant. The concept is interchangeable with 'the flowers of the deep regions of the forest'.
4. 'Early harvest' – this is a very important and special crop often taken from a special garden. It is shared ceremonially with very close friends.
5. The man-eater bird is a mythological bird that steals people so long as it can find them in isolation but it can easily be scared away from its prey by a crowd.
6. Lizard – this creature symbolizes death. It is said when God created mankind, he decided to send a chameleon to tell people on earth that they shall live eternally. But later he changed his mind and sent a lizard (speed) who outran the chameleon with its death message.
7. 'Clan of the Black bird' – this refers to the same concept of fertility and power as associated with the season of decay, rejuvenation and potential. This precedes and predetermines the season of the great harvest and 'fruitfulness'.
8. The sun is central in many African mythologies, playing the generative and procreative role.
9. 'Green Mushrooms' – this symbolizes the idea of growth and cleansing.
10. In every era are born the children of the sun. These are very special

people. They are not necessarily the happiest of people. Their greatest suffering comes from the suffering of others. They are often pained by the contemporary since they live far beyond their time. It is this quality that makes them beautiful in the sense of an inner excellence and serenity.

The Contributors

RICHARD ACLAND is a former Labour M.P. who resigned over the issue of the British manufacture of the H-Bomb. During the second world war, after commencing his parliamentary career as a Liberal, he became leader of the Common Wealth Party. After his retirement from politics he devoted himself to education and was on the staff of St. Luke's College, Exeter. He is the author of several books.

EDWARD CARPENTER is Vice-President of Christian Action and has been the Dean of Westminster Abbey since 1974, having been a member of the chapter of the Abbey for a quarter of a century. He is also the author of many books on theology and church history.

THOMAS CORBISHLEY, who died prior to the publication of this volume, was a distinguished Roman Catholic priest and member of the Society of Jesus. He was for many years Master of Campion Hall, Oxford and the author of many theological and devotional works.

JACQUETTA HAWKES is an archaeologist and the author of several books and plays. Like her husband J. B. Priestley she was a leading activist in the Campaign for Nuclear Disarmament.

IAN HENDERSON is on the Council of Christian Action and is Vicar of the Ascension, Ealing in west London. He is also Chaplain for Social Responsibility to the Bishop of Willesden and was Executive Officer of Christian Action from 1964 to 1970.

TREVOR HUDDLESTON, a member of the Anglican Community of the Resurrection, is Bishop of Stepney in the Diocese of London, having served for many years in Africa, first as Prior of his Community's house in Johannesburg and later as Bishop of Masasi. In the former capacity he became world-renowned as an opponent of apartheid.

MERVYN JONES is a journalist and novelist who has been associated with many radical and socialist causes. He was active in the

Campaign for Nuclear Disarmament and was one of the leading opponents of Great Britain's entry into the EEC.

RAYMOND KUNENE is an African poet who now lives in exile. He has played a leading role in the African nationalist movement.

THE EARL OF LONGFORD, a well-known author and broadcaster, is a member of a distinguished Anglo-Irish family and was known as Baron Pakenham until succeeding to his brother's title. He served in the post-war Labour governments under Clement Attlee, and has been associated with Christian Action since its foundation.

IRIS MURDOCH is a novelist, playwright and philosopher of international acclaim whose play *A Severed Head* had a long, successful run on the London stage. She has been active in many public and humanitarian causes.

J. B. PRIESTLEY, a doyen of English novelists and playwrights, first received national critical attention in 1929 with his novel *The Good Companions*. He has been active in many humanitarian and radical causes over the years in company with his wife Jacquetta Hawkes.

JOSEPH ROBINSON is a canon of Canterbury Cathedral who was for many years a minor canon of St. Paul's. He is an Old Testament scholar who has lectured at London University and is a regular contributor to the religious press.

PER WASTBERG is one of Sweden's most successful younger novelists and is chief editor of that country's principal daily newspaper. He is President of Swedish PEN and was one of the founders of the Swedish branch of the International Defence and Aid Fund for Southern Africa.